Library of Congress Catalog Number: 72-116065
International Standard Book Number: 0-379-12074-7

Manufactured in the United States of America

WILLIAM McKINLEY
1843 - 1901

Chronology - Documents - Bibliographical Aids

Edited by
HARRY J. SIEVERS, S. J.
Professor of History
Fordham University

Series Editor
Howard F. Bremer

1970
OCEANA PUBLICATIONS, INC.
Dobbs Ferry, New York

CONTENTS ⏜105771

EDITOR'S FOREWORD

In this Chronology every attempt has been made to cite the most accurate dates. Diaries, letters, newspapers, official documents, and similar evidence have been used to determine the exact date. In some few instances where conflicting evidence appeared, the more plausible date has been chosen.

This volume is primarily a research tool intended for the ready and facile use of collegians and graduate students interested in the History of the Presidency. Obviously, any selection of "significant events" or "key documents" implies arbitrary and subjective judgment. It is believed, however, that such choices are reasonable insofar as they reflect an acquaintance with the McKinley era and with the Presidential papers involved.

The purpose of this book is threefold: 1) to make readily available the pertinent facts in McKinley's career; 2) to provide the key documents, official and unofficial, that reflect the President's role in American History; 3) to present a critical bibliography that can both guide and stimulate students to further research. Although many titles recommended may not always be available in smaller libraries, yet a majority of the bibliographical aids can now be secured in paperback editions.

Documents in this volume are reproduced from several standard sources. Grateful acknowledgment is made to the following collections: James D. Richardson, Messages and Papers of the Presidents; The President Speaks: From William McKinley to Lyndon B. Johnson (edited with an Introduction by Louis Filler); The Annals of America, Vol. XII; Henry Steele Commager, Documents in American History; American Democracy: A Documentary Record, Vol. II, 1865-1961 (edited by J. Rogers Hollingsworth and Bell I. Wiley); [U.S. Department of State] Papers Relating to Foreign Affairs.

CHRONOLOGY

CHRONOLOGY

1843

January 29   Born: Niles, Ohio. Father: William McKinley. Mother: Nancy Campbell Allison.

1852-1859

Family moved to Poland, near Youngstown, Ohio. Attended public schools and graduated from Poland Academy at 17; joined Methodist Church, the religion of his mother.

1860

Autumn   Entered Allegheny College at Meadville, Pennsylvania; joined Sigma Alpha Epsilon. Fell ill at end of first term and withdrew.

1861

Winter and Spring   Taught school and clerked in post office at Poland.

April 14   Fort Sumter fell.

June   Enlisted as private in the 23rd Regiment, Ohio Volunteer Infantry; at Columbus was mustered in for three years "or the duration."

September   Saw action in western Virginia; exemplary conduct noted by Lieutenant Colonel Rutherford B. Hayes.

1862

April 15   Made commissary sergeant; regiment ordered to Washington and attached to Army of the Potomac.

September 17   Served in Battle of Antietam.

September 24   Commissioned second lieutenant.

1

Autumn   Enjoyed only leave during the war.

1863

February 7   Promoted to first lieutenant; closely associated with
                  Hayes who described him as "one of the bravest and
                  finest officers in the Army."

1864

July 25   Advanced to captain; became expert horseman; was
                  officially commended for gallantry in Shenandoah
                  Valley campaign.

November   Cast first vote for Lincoln.

1865

March 13   Became brevet major of volunteers.

July 26   Mustered out after four years of service.

Autumn.   Read law in office of local Ohio attorney.

1866

Fall   Commenced studies in law school, Albany, New York.

1867

Spring   Admitted to bar in Warren, Ohio, and set up law
                  practice at Canton, Ohio, the seat of Stark County
                  and the home of his sister, Anna; joined Masons,
                  Y.M.C.A., and was superintendent of Sunday School
                  of the First Methodist Church.

Autumn   Appeared on hustings; supported successful bid of
                  Rutherford B. Hayes for governorship.

1868

Summer and   Formed U.S. Grant-for-President clubs; was elected
Fall   prosecuting attorney of Stark County, a traditional
                  Democratic stronghold.

1869-1871

As prosecuting attorney warred successfully against the illicit sale of liquor; met and courted Ida Saxton, daughter of a Canton businessman and banker.

1871

January 24
Married Ida Saxton at Canton.

December 25
Daughter Katherine born; named for Ida's mother.

1872

Summer and Fall
Campaigned for re-election of President Grant.

1873

March 31
Daughter Ida born but lived less than five months; wife stricken and remained a crippled invalid for life.

August 23
Death of baby Ida McKinley (5 months).

1874-1875

Expanded law practice in Canton; supported Hayes' third campaign for governorship.

1875

July 25
Death of first-born Katherine (3 1/2 years); domestic tragedies continue.

1876

Summer
Supported R. B. Hayes for presidency; announced own candidacy for Congress.

Autumn
Won seat in Congress.

CONGRESSIONAL CAREER

1877

March 4
Member of 45th Congress from Ohio; lodged at Ebbitt House; specialized on the tariff; maintained close

relations with President and Mrs. Hayes; initial salary
of $5,000.

1879

March 4
Member of 46th Congress; strongly supported protective tariff as sound national policy; grew in public stat-
ure; rewarded by appointment to House Ways and Means
Committee.

1880

June 2-5, 7-8
Chaired Committee on Resolutions at 7th Republican
National Convention in Chicago; supported candidacy
of John Sherman; gained friendship of Marcus A. Hanna.

1881

March 4
Member of 47th Congress.

1883

March 4
Presented credentials as member-elect of 48th Congress and was seated.

1884

May 27
Succeeded in House by J. H. Wallace who successfully
contested his re-election in 1882.

June 3-6
Attended Republican National Convention in Chicago.

1885

March 4
Again elected to Congress and served in the 49th, 50th
and 51st Congresses (through March 3, 1891).

1886

September 15
Encouraged future President Benjamin Harrison to seek
second term in U.S. Senate.

1888

February 22
Attended annual Michigan Club Banquet in Detroit;
cheered "rejuvenated Republican" Harrison as next
GOP presidential candidate.

June 19-23	Active role at Republican National Convention in Chicago; as "an aroused protectionist" from Ohio, read party platform to convention. It was styled a "complete handbook of Republicanism"; regarded as "dark horse" hopeful; nominated but withdrew name from ballot in favor of John Sherman.
October 25	Supported Harrison's canvass with key appearance at Indianapolis rally.

1889

February	Considered by President-elect Harrison for Secretary of Treasury.
July	Visited summer White House at Deer Park, Maryland; speculated on being elected Speaker of the House of Representatives.
December	Party caucus selected Thomas B. Reed of Maine as Speaker; named McKinley chairman of Ways and Means Committee - a useful stepping-stone.

1890

Summer	Sponsored controversial tariff legislation that sparked long debate.
July	Accompanied Harrison to G.A.R. Encampment in Boston.
September 10	Senate passes own version of McKinley tariff bill.
October 1	Harrison signed McKinley tariff and reciprocity legislation, shaking the Ohioan's hand.
November	Unsuccessful candidate for re-election to Congress. Democratic gerrymander helped to end 14 years in the House.

GUBERNATORIAL CAREER (1891-1896)

1891

March 3   Left Washington for Canton.

June   Nominated by acclamation as Ohio's GOP gubernatorial candidate.

Fall   Campaigned solely on national issues of a sound currency and a protective tariff; elected governor by a plurality of 25,500 votes.

1892

January   Inaugurated governor of Ohio; pledged public welfare and condemned gerrymander; urged tax reforms and new labor laws.

April   At convention of Republican League Clubs in Cincinnati spoke for Harrison's renomination despite heavy sentiment for Blaine.

June 7-10   Attended GOP National Convention at Minneapolis as favorite son candidate from Ohio; served as permanent chairman; got Ohio's 44 votes but recorded himself for Harrison who was renominated on first ballot.

June 20   Headed committee to notify Harrison in Washington that he had won renomination unanimously.

1893

Fall   Won second term as governor.

1894

Autumn   Campaigned in 16 states for Republican congressional candidates. Made 371 speeches whose theme was "Protection, Patriotism, and Prosperity." Credited with major role in effecting a GOP sweep, especially in northern states.

1895

Winter   Spent winter 1894-95 in Thomasville, Georgia. Here
                  Mark Hanna began to line up southern support for a
                  McKinley nomination in 1896.

Late Spring   Addressed banquet in Hartford, Connecticut, where
                  J. Addison Porter, a wealthy newspaper owner, formed
                  a "McKinley for President" club. It soon stimulated
                  similar organizations throughout the nation.

Fall   Campaigned indefatigably to elect Republican Asa A.
                  Bushnell to Ohio governorship. Then declared per-
                  sonal moratorium on politics until national convention
                  of 1896. Awarded Ll.D. by Allegheny College.

CAMPAIGN FOR PRESIDENCY

1896

February   Noted Benjamin Harrison's withdrawal as a presidential
                  candidate and regarded Czar Thomas B. Reed as only
                  serious rival for GOP nomination.

February 12   Addressed Marquette Club in Chicago and outlined "Mc-
                  Kinleyism." Only 1896 speech delivered outside of
                  Canton, Ohio. Resumed campaign of silence.

March   Ohio Republican Convention endorsed McKinley and
                  triggered a national trend.

April 28   Backing by Illinois Republicans is regarded as decisive
                  in pre-convention maneuvering. Attacks by American
                  Protective Association (APA) ignored by McKinley.

June 9   J. H. Manley of Maine predicts a first ballot nomina-
                  tion for the man from Ohio.

June 16   Republican Convention opened at St. Louis. McKinley
                  remained at Canton.

June 18	Chosen on first ballot with 661 1/2 votes to 84 1/2 for Thomas B. Reed. Nomination by acclamation followed. Garret a. Hobart of New Jersey named as vice presidential candidate.
July 7-11	Democratic Convention met in Chicago. William Jennings Bryan of Nebraska nominated on fifth ballot. Acclamation makes choice unanimous. Arthur Sewall of Maine selected as vice presidential running mate.
Summer	At Canton conducted a "front porch" campaign receiving visitors and delegations at all hours every day except Sunday. Aided by a volume of broadsides and political pamphlets known as the "literary campaign."
July	Address to McKinley-Hobart Club of Knoxville styled as "good as gold speech," used to offset Bryan's "Cross of Gold" speech.
August	Read formal Letter of Acceptance. Endorsed gold-standard plank and stressed patriotism, protection, and prosperity.
Autumn	Shifted emphasis from "free silver" issue to prosperity through economic nationalism.
Election Day-November 5	Polled largest majority since Grant's 1872 victory; 7,104,779 popular votes for McKinley; 6,502,925 for Bryan. McKinley received 65.33 percent (292 electoral votes - 28 states) to Bryan's 34.67 percent (155 electoral votes - 17 states).

TERM OF OFFICE

1897

February	Publicly announced Cabinet slate as follows: John Sherman as Secretary of State; Russell A. Alger as Secretary of War; Lyman Gage as Secretary of Treasury; James A. Gay as Postmaster General; John Long as Secretary of Navy; James Wilson as Secretary of Agriculture; Joseph McKenna as Attorney General;

Cornelius N. Bliss as Secretary of Interior.

March 1	Left Canton for Washington with some fifty relatives and friends.
March 2	Arrived in Washington; dined with Grover Cleveland; styled White House interview as one of "settled sadness"; expressed conviction that he could keep nation at peace.
March 4	Inaugurated as 25th President, his nearly 4,000 word address stressed government revenue and promised legislation aimed at aiding business.
March 15	Called Congress into special session to draft a new protective tariff and to revise currency legislation.
March 31	Helped to draft Dingley Tariff Bill that passed the House of Representatives 205-122.
April 12	Appointed special commission to study prospects for international bimetallism.
June 6	Submitted to Senate treaty to annex Hawaii.
July 7	Dingley Tariff passed by Senate.
July 24	Signed into law as the highest tariff to date.
Fall	Prospects for international silver agreement declined.
December 12	Mother, Nancy Campbell Allison McKinley, died, Canton, Ohio.
December 24	Cuban Relief Committee sought public contributions; McKinley sent anonymous gift of $5,000.

1898

January	Cuban unrest moved McKinley to alert Navy.

January 24	Battleship U.S.S. Maine sent to Havana, cruiser U.S.S. Montgomery to Santiago and Matanzas, as a mark of friendship and international courtesy.
February 9	New York Journal published de Lome letter describing McKinley as weak. Anti-Spanish sentiment in U.S. so increased that Spanish Minister to U.S. de Lome resigned.
February 15	U.S.S. Maine wracked by explosion in Havana harbor. "Remember the Maine" becomes cry of interventionists.
February 22	At University of Pennsylvania address he called for sober public judgment and good faith toward all nations.
March 8	Bill introduced in House appropriating $50 million for national defense, passed by Senate the following day.
March 20	Board of Inquiry's report unanimous - the U.S.S. Maine had been blown up by a submarine mine.
March 21-26	Conferred with members of Congress and Cabinet on growing tensions.
March 27	Despite mounting war fever in the United States, the President worked for peace, instructing Minister Stewart Woodford to deny U.S. desire to annex Cuba.
March 28	Report on U.S.S. Maine sent to Congress.
March 29	Ultimatum sent to Spain calling for immediate cessation of hostilities.
April 6	Diplomatic Corps urged President to maintain peace.
April 9	McKinley informed of papal efforts and of other powers to preserve peace. Spain agreed to U.S. demand to stop brutalities in Cuba.

April 11	Goaded by public and political pressure, reversed anti-war policy and asked for congressional resolution authorizing use of Army and Navy to force Spain to leave Cuba and declare Cuba independent.
April 19	Both houses adopted Senate resolutions.
April 20	Signed resolution passed by Congress, but Spain broke diplomatic relations before U.S. ultimatum could be delivered.
April 22	Ordered blockade of Cuban ports and authorized a volunteer force of 200,000 to build up Army that numbered only 28,000 men and 2,100 officers.
April 24	Instructed Dewey in Hong Kong to proceed to Philippines and "commence" operations.
April 25	Formal declaration of war after Spanish rejection of ultimatum. Made retroactive to April 21.
May 1	Admiral Dewey crippled 10 ships at Manila Bay, Philippines, in seven-hour battle that resulted in more than 300 Spanish deaths and 7 wounded for U.S.
May 2	American troops mobilized and sent to Philippines.
May 19	Spanish Atlantic fleet arrived in harbor of Santiago de Cuba.
May 29	U.S. naval force from Key West blocked entrance to Santiago, bottling up Spanish ships.
June 6	Santiago forts withstand heavy bombardment.
June 8	17,000 soldiers moved into Tampa for embarkation to Santiago.
June 10	Congress passed War Revenue Bill.

June 14	Fleet finally cleared for Cuba.
June 15	600 Marines defeated Spanish in Battle of Guantanamo Bay.
June 22	Fleet arrived in Cuba, carrying 17,000 troops under General William Shafter.
July 1	Theodore Roosevelt led attack on San Juan Hill.
July 3	Spanish tried to run U.S. blockade; lost fleet and suffered 2,000 killed.
July 7	Signed joint resolution of Congress annexing Hawaii.
July 17	Santiago's 24,000 defenders surrendered to U.S.
July 21	In last Cuban sea battle of the war, four U.S. ships bombarded and captured Nipo.
July 25	American expedition sent to subdue Puerto Rico. General Wesley Merritt reinforced Manila blockade with land forces.
July 30	Peace protocol transmitted by U.S. to Spanish government through French ambassador.
July 31	Hostilities suspended by proclamation.
August 10	Spanish agree to terms.
August 12	Protocol signed and fighting ceased. Problem of Philippines postponed until formal peace conference.
August 13-14	Unaware that hostilities were over, U.S. battled Filipino guerrillas and forced the surrender of Manila.
August 26	Five-man commission appointed to negotiate peace with Spain.

Early September	President McKinley visited wounded veterans at Montauk Point.
September 12	Formally instructed peace commissioners en route to Paris.
October 1	Peace commission met in Paris; with public opinion on Philippines still divided; President demanded cession of Islands to U.S.
October	McKinley stumped Midwest and West in support of Republican congressional candidates.
October 26	Commission is instructed to take the Philippine Islands.
November 28	Spanish peace commissioners finally agreed to following terms: 1) cession of the Philippine Islands for payment of $20 million; 2) surrender of all claims to Cuba, making it independent; 3) Spanish assumption of Cuban public debt of $400 million; 4) cession of Guam and Puerto Rico to U.S.
December 10	Treaty of Paris signed, marking end of Spanish rule in Western Hemisphere.
Mid-December	McKinley toured the southern states.

                                    1899

January 4	Treaty of Paris transmitted to the Senate.
January 5	Independent Philippine Republic declared under Aguinaldo.
February 4	Filipino guerrillas unsuccessfully battle U.S. forces in Luzon.
February 6	Treaty of Paris ratified by the Senate after heated debate between imperialists and anti-imperialists.

February 16   Before the Home Market Club in Boston, McKinley's speech marked first anniversary of the sinking of the U.S.S. Maine.

February 17   Anti-Imperialist League founded to oppose territorial expansion beyond continental limits of the U.S.A.

March   U.S. campaign launched against Filipino guerrillas; some 70,000 troops engaged on each side.

April 11   Philippines, Puerto Rico, and Guam formally acquired by United States.

May 18   U.S. attended disarmament and arbitration conference at The Hague.

July   Old McKinley home in Canton, Ohio, is re-sold to the President.

August 1   Accepted resignation of War Secretary Russell A. Alger (effective January 2, 1900); named Elihu Root of New York as successor.
                 Spent month vacationing at Lake Champlain.

September   Ordered 35,000 additional troops to Philippine Islands.

September 6   Made public Secretary of State John Hay's circular letter proclaiming an "Open Door" policy towards China.

October   White House reception for Admiral Dewey.

Fall   Hit campaign trail in western states, including the Dakotas.

November 7-   Republicans won 8 of 12 state elections.
Election Day

November 21   Death of Vice President Garret A. Hobart.

December 2   American Samoa acquired by treaty; U.S. formally
                  claimed Wake Island, an atoll in the Central Pacific
                  Ocean, for use as a cable station.

December   Annual message to Congress stressed presidential con-
                  trol over colonial policy in the Philippines; called for
                  an end of military occupation, followed by independence
                  as soon as Filipinos were capable of self-government.

                              1900

January   Senator Albert J. Beveridge, young Republican expan-
                  sionist, declared Philippines were U.S. territory by
                  act of God and should be retained. McKinley unim-
                  pressed by imperialistic rhetoric.

March 4   Fifty-sixth Congress convened; Republicans in full con-
                  trol for the first time since 1889.

March 14   Congress passed Gold Standard Act, making gold the
                  only currency standard in the U.S.

March 20   John Hay announced that Germany, Russia, Britain,
                  France, Italy, and Japan had accepted "Open Door"
                  policy for China.

April   Admiral Dewey announced his presidential candidacy;
                  failed to gain major support.

April 7   President appointed a second Philippine Commission
                  headed by Federal Circuit Judge William Howard Taft
                  to establish civil government in the Islands.

April 12   McKinley signed Foraker Bill, creating civil govern-
                  ment for Puerto Rico and extending Dingley Tariff to in-
                  clude the island.

May 1   Charles H. Allen became first American civil governor
                  of Puerto Rico.

May 10   Fusion Populist Party nominated William Jennings Bryan
                  for President.

June 19   Republican National Convention opened in Philadelphia, Pennsylvania.

June 21   McKinley renominated on the first ballot with 926 votes, later made unanimous. Theodore Roosevelt of New York was nominated for Vice President.

Summer   Repeated pattern of first campaign, never leaving Canton, but Roosevelt covered 21,000 miles, made 700 speeches and often wore his "Rough Rider" hat.

July 3   Peking, China, occupied by local groups known as Boxers. Secretary of State Hay circularized U.S. desire for a solution to bring permanent safety and peace to China.

July 4-6   At Kansas City, Missouri, Democratic National Convention nominated William Jennings Bryan for President and Adlai E. Stevenson for Vice President on an anti-imperialist and free silver platform.

July 12   McKinley responded to formal notification of renomination with his only speech of the campaign, alleging it improper for a President "of all the people" to contend for re-election on a partisan basis.

August 14   United States joined international expeditionary force to crush Boxer Rebellion in Peking.

September 1   By executive order Taft Commission is constituted as the legislative body of the Filipino archipelago.

November 6- Republican candidates received 7,207,923 popular votes
Election Day (65.33 percent) and 292 electoral votes (28 states). Bryan and Stevenson received 6,358,138 popular votes (34.67 percent) and 155 electoral votes (17 states).

SECOND PRESIDENTIAL TERM

1901

January	Heavy cold and grippe confine President to bed - his only serious illness in the White House.
January 24	United States signed treaty with Denmark for purchase of Danish West Indies; Danish Parliament rejected it.
March 2	Platt Amendment passed by Congress. Its more important provisions were: 1) Cuba would never enter into any treaty with any foreign power impairing Cuban independence; 2) the Cuban government would not contract any public debt in excess of the capacity of its ordinary revenues to discharge; 3) U.S. was authorized to intervene to preserve Cuban independence and maintain law and order; and 4) Cuba agreed to sell or lease to the U.S. lands necessary for naval or coaling stations.
March 4	First inauguration of 20th century and centenary of first inauguration held in the Federal District.
April 19- June 13	National tour planned in an effort to win support for trust-busting and for extending commercial reciprocity.
May	Supreme Court decided that the U.S. had the right to acquire territory by treaty but concluded that the Constitution did not automatically extend to the territory so acquired.
June 11	McKinley dismissed talk of a third term.
July 4	Taft assumed executive power from military governor of Philippines; the insurrection of Aguinaldo ended.
July 5	McKinley left to spend summer at Canton.
September 5	At Pan American Exposition in Buffalo, New York,

vigorously recommended broad policy of commercial
reciprocity.

September 6   Following an excursion to Niagara Falls, President
attended reception at Temple of Music. Here profes-
sional anarchist Leon Czolgosz fired two shots into
McKinley at close range.

September 7-14 After an operation there followed a series of rallies
and relapses. On the 14th death came. "Nearer my
God to Thee" were President McKinley's last words.

September 14   Theodore Roosevelt was sworn in as 26th President.

DOCUMENTS

DOCUMENTS

INAUGURAL ADDRESS
March 4, 1897

Fellow-Citizens:

In obedience to the will of the people, and in their presence, by the authority vested in me by this oath, I assume the arduous and responsible duties of President of the United States, relying upon the support of my countrymen and invoking the guidance of Almighty God. Our faith teaches that there is no safer reliance than upon the God of our fathers, who has so singularly favored the American people in every national trial, and who will not forsake us so long as we obey His commandments and walk humbly in His footsteps.

The responsibilities of the high trust to which I have been called — always of grave importance — are augmented by the prevailing business conditions entailing idleness upon willing labor and loss to useful enterprises. The country is suffering from industrial disturbances from which speedy relief must be had. Our financial system needs some revision; our money is all good now, but its value must not further be threatened. It should all be put upon an enduring basis, not subject to easy attack, nor its stability to doubt or dispute. Our currency should continue under the supervision of the Government. The several forms of our paper money offer, in my judgment, a constant embarrassment to the Government and a safe balance in the Treasury. Therefore I believe it necessary to devise a system which, without diminishing the circulating medium or offering a premium for its contraction, will present a remedy for those arrangements which, temporary in their nature, might well in the years of our prosperity have been displaced by wiser provisions. With adequate revenue secured, but not until then, we can enter upon such changes in our fiscal laws as will, while insuring safety and volume to our money, no longer impose upon the Government the necessity of maintaining so large a gold reserve, with its attendant and inevitable temptations to speculation. Most of óur financial laws are the outgrowth of experience and trial, and should not be amended without investigation and demonstration of the wisdom of the proposed changes. We must be both "sure we are right" and "make haste slowly." If, therefore, Congress, in its wisdom, shall deem it expedient to create a commission to take under early consideration the revision of our coinage, banking and currency laws, and give them that exhaustive, careful dispassionate examination that their importance demands, I shall cordially concur in such action. If such power is vested in the President, it is my purpose to appoint a commission of prominent, well-informed citizens of different parties, who will command public confidence, both on account of their ability and special fitness for the work. Business experience and public training may thus be combined, and the patriotic zeal of the friends of the country be so directed that such a report will be made as to receive the support of all parties, and our finances cease to be the subject of mere partisan contention. The experiment is, at all events, worth a trial, and, in my opinion, it can but prove beneficial to the entire country.

The question of international bimetallism will have early and earnest attention. It will be my constant endeavor to secure it by cooperation with the other great commercial powers of the world. Until that condition is realized when the parity between our gold and silver money springs from and is supported by the relative value of the two metals, the value of the silver already coined and of that which may hereafter be coined, must be kept constantly at par with gold by every resource at our command. The credit of the Government, the integrity of its currency, and the inviolability of its obligations must be preserved. This was the commanding verdict of the people, and it will not be unheeded.

Economy is demanded in every branch of the Government at all times, but especially in periods, like the present, of depression in business and distress among the people. The severest economy must be observed in all public expenditures, and extravagance stopped wherever it is found, and prevented wherever in the future it may be developed. If the revenues are to remain as now, the only relief that can come must be from decreased expenditures. But the present must not become the permanent condition of the Government. It has been our uniform practice to retire, not increase our outstanding obligations, and this policy must again be resumed and vigorously enforced. Our revenues should always be large enough to meet with ease and promptness not only our current needs and the principal and interest of the public debt, but to make proper and liberal provision for that most deserving body of public creditors, the soldiers and sailors and the widows and orphans who are the pensioners of the United States.

The Government should not be permitted to run behind or increase its debt in times like the present. Suitably to provide against this is the mandate of duty — the certain and easy remedy for most of our financial difficulties. A deficiency is inevitable so long as the expenditures of the Government exceed its receipts. It can only be met by loans or an increased revenue. While a large annual surplus of revenue may invite waste and extravagance, inadequate revenue creates distrust and undermines public and private credit. Neither should be encouraged. Between more loans and more revenue there ought to be but one opinion. We should have more revenue, and that without delay, hindrance, or postponement. A surplus in the Treasury created by loans is not a permanent or safe reliance. It will suffice while it lasts, but it can not last long while the outlays of the Government are greater than its receipts, as has been the case during the past two years. Nor must it be forgotten that however much such loans may temporarily relieve the situation, the Government is still indebted for the amount of the surplus thus accrued, which it must ultimately pay, while its ability to pay is not strengthened, but weakened by a continued deficit. Loans are imperative in great emergencies to preserve the Government or its credit, but a failure to supply needed revenue in time of peace for the maintenance of either has no justification.

The best way for the Government to maintain its credit is to pay as it goes — not by resorting to loans, but by keeping out of debt — through an adequate income secured by a system of taxation, external or internal, or both. It is the settled policy of the Government, pursued from the beginning and practised by all parties and Administrations, to raise the bulk of our revenue from taxes upon foreign productions entering the United States for sale and consumption, and avoiding, for the most part, every form of direct taxation, except in time of war. The country is clearly opposed to any needless additions to the subject of internal taxation, and is committed by its latest popular utterance to the system of tariff taxation. There can be no misunderstanding, either, about the principle upon which this tariff taxation shall be levied. Nothing has ever been made plainer at a general election than that the controlling principle in the raising of revenue from duties on imports is zealous care for American interests and American labor. The people have declared that such legislation should be had as will give ample protection and encouragement to the industries and the development of our country. It is, therefore, earnestly hoped and expected that Congress will, at the earliest practicable moment, enact revenue legislation that shall be fair, reasonable, conservative, and just, and which, while supplying sufficient revenue for public purposes, will still be signally beneficial and helpful to every section and every enterprise of the people. To this policy we are all, of whatever party, firmly bound by the voice of the people — a power vastly more potential than the expression of any political platform. The paramount duty of Congress is to stop deficiencies by the restoration of that protective legislation which has always been the firmest prop of the Treasury. The passage of such a law or laws would strengthen the credit of the Government both at home and abroad, and go far toward stopping the drain upon the gold reserve held for the redemption of our currency, which has been heavy and well-nigh constant for several years.

In the revision of the tariff especial attention should be given to the re-enactment and extension of the reciprocity principle of the law of 1890, under which so great a stimulus was given to our foreign trade in new and advantageous markets for our surplus agricultural and manufactured products. The brief trial given this legislation amply justifies a further experiment and additional discretionary power in the making of commercial treaties, the end in view always to be the opening up of new markets for the products of our country, by granting concessions to the products of other lands that we need and cannot produce ourselves, and which do not involve any loss of labor to our own people, but tend to increase their employment.

The depression of the past four years has fallen with especial severity upon the great body of toilers of the country, and upon none more than the holders of small farms. Agriculture has languished and labor suffered. The revival of manufacturing will be a relief to both. No portion of our population is more devoted to the institution of free government nor more loyal in their support, while none bears more cheerfully or fully its proper share in the maintenance of the Government or is better entitled to its wise and liberal care and protection. Legislation helpful to producers is beneficial to all. The depressed condition of industry on the farm and in the mine and factory has lessened the ability of the people to meet the demands upon them, and they rightfully expect that not only a system of revenue shall be established that will secure the largest income with the least burden, but that every means will be taken to decrease, rather than increase, our public expenditures. Business conditions are not the most promising. It will take time to restore the prosperity of former years. If we cannot promptly attain it, we can resolutely turn our faces in that direction and aid its return by friendly legislation. However troublesome the situation may appear, Congress will not, I am sure, be found lacking in disposition or ability to relieve it as far as legislation can do so. The restoration of confidence and the revival of business, which men of all parties so much desire, depend more largely upon the prompt, energetic, and intelligent action of Congress than upon any other single agency affecting the situation.

It is inspiring, too, to remember that no great emergency in the one hundred and eight years of our eventful national life has ever arisen that has not been met with wisdom and courage by the American people, with fidelity to their best interests and highest destiny, and to the honor of the American name. These years of glorious history have exalted mankind and advanced the cause of freedom throughout the world, and immeasurably strengthened the precious free institutions which we enjoy. The people love and will sustain these institutions. The great essential to our happiness and prosperity is that we adhere to the principles upon which the Government was established and insist upon their faithful observance. Equality of rights must prevail, and our laws be always and everywhere respected and obeyed. We may have failed in the discharge of our full duty as citizens of the great Republic, but it is consoling and encouraging to realize that free speech, a free press, free thought, free schools, the free and unmolested right of religious liberty and worship, and free and fair elections are dearer and more universally enjoyed to-day than ever before. These guaranties must be sacredly preserved and wisely strengthened. The constituted authorities must be cheerfully and vigorously upheld. Lynchings must not be tolerated in a great and civilized country like the United States; courts, not mobs, must execute the penalties of the law. The preservation of public order, the right of discussion, the integrity of courts, and the orderly administration of justice must continue forever the rock of safety upon which our Government securely rests.

One of the lessons taught by the late election, which all can rejoice in, is that the citizens of the United States are both law-respecting and law-abiding people, not easily swerved from the path of patriotism and honor. This is in entire accord with the genius of our institutions, and but emphasizes the advantages of inculcating even a greater love for law and order in the future. Immunity should be granted to none who violate the laws, whether individuals, corporations, or communities; and as the Constitution imposes upon the President the duty of both its own execution, and of the statutes enacted in pursuance of its provisions, I shall endeavor carefully to carry them into effect. The declaration of the party now restored to power has been in the past that of "opposition to all combinations of capital organized in trusts, or otherwise, to control arbitrarily the condition of trade among our citizens," and it has supported "such legislation as will prevent the execution of all schemes to oppress the people by undue charges on their supplies, or by unjust rates for the transportation of their products to the market." This purpose will be steadily pursued, both by the enforcement of the laws now in existence and the recommendation and support of such new statutes as may be necessary to carry it into effect.

Our naturalization and immigration laws should be further improved to the constant promotion of a safer, a better, and a higher citizenship. A grave peril to the Republic would be a citizenship too ignorant to understand or too vicious to appreciate the great value and beneficence of our institutions and laws, and against all who come here to make war upon them our gates must be promptly and tightly closed. Nor must we be unmindful of the need of improvement among our own citizens, but with the zeal of our forefathers encourage the spread of knowledge and free education. Illiteracy must be banished from the land if we shall attain that high destiny as the foremost of the enlightened nations of the world which, under Providence, we ought to achieve.

Reforms in the civil service must go on; but the changes should be real and genuine, not perfunctory, or prompted by a zeal in behalf of any party simply because it happens to be in power. As a member of Congress I voted and spoke in favor of the present law, and I shall attempt its enforcement in the spirit in which it was enacted. The purpose in view was to secure the most efficient service of the best men who would accept appointment under the Government, retaining faithful and devoted public servants in office, but shielding none, under the authority of any rule or custom, who are inefficient, incompetent, or unworthy. The best interests of the country demand this, and the people heartily approve the law wherever and whenever it has been thus administrated.

Congress should give prompt attention to the restoration of our American merchant marine, once the pride of the seas in all the great ocean highways of commerce. To my mind, few more important subjects so imperatively demand its intelligent consideration. The United States has progressed with marvelous rapidity in every field of enterprise and endeavor until we have become foremost in nearly all the great lines of inland trade, commerce, and industry. Yet, while this is true, our American merchant marine has been steadily declining until it is now lower, both in the percentage of tonnage and the number of vessels employed, than it was prior to the Civil War. Commendable progress has been made of late years in the upbuilding of the American Navy, but we must supplement these efforts by providing as a proper consort for it a merchant marine amply sufficient for our own carrying trade to foreign countries. The question is one that appeals both to our business necessities and the patriotic aspirations of a great people.

It has been the policy of the United States since the foundation of the Government to cultivate relations of peace and amity with all the nations of the world, and this accords with my conception of our duty now. We have cherished the policy of non-interference with affairs of foreign governments wisely inaugurated by Washington, keeping ourselves free from entanglement, either as allies or foes, content to leave undisturbed with them the settlement of their own domestic concerns. It will be our aim to pursue a firm and dignified foreign policy, which shall be just, impartial, ever watchful of our national honor, and always insisting upon the enforcement of the lawful rights of American citizens everywhere. Our diplomacy should seek nothing more and accept nothing less than is due us. We want no wars of conquest; we must avoid the temptation of territorial aggression. War should never be entered upon until every agency of peace has failed; peace is preferable to war in almost every contingency. Arbitration is the true method of settlement of international as well as local or individual differences. It was recognized as the best means of adjustment of differences between employers and employees by the Forty-ninth Congress, in 1886, and its application was extended to our diplomatic relations by the unanimous concurrence of the Senate and House of the Fifty-first Congress in 1890. The latter resolution was accepted as the basis of negotiations with us by the British House of Commons in 1893, and upon our invitation a treaty of arbitration between the United States and Great Britain was signed at Washington and transmitted to the Senate for its ratification in January last. Since this treaty is clearly the result of our own initiative; since it has been recognized as the leading feature of our foreign policy throughout our entire national history — the adjustment of difficulties by judicial methods rather than force of arms — and since it presents to the world the glorious example of reason and peace, not passion and war, controlling the relations between two of the greatest nations in the world, an example certain to be followed by others, I respectfully urge the early action of the Senate thereon, not merely as a matter of policy, but as a duty to mankind. The importance and moral influence of the ratification of such a treaty can hardly be overestimated in the cause of advancing civilization. It may well engage the best thought of the statesmen and people of every country, and I cannot but consider it fortunate that it was reserved to the United States to have the leadership in so grand a work.

It has been the uniform practice of each President to avoid, as far as possible, the convening of Congress in extraordinary session. It is an example which, under ordinary circumstances and in the absence of a public necessity, is to be commended. But a failure to convene the representatives of the people in Congress in extra session when it involves neglect of a public duty places the responsibility of such neglect upon the Executive himself. The condition of the public Treasury, as has been indicated, demands the immediate consideration of Congress. It alone has the power to provide revenues for the Government. Not to convene it under such circumstances I can view in no other sense than the neglect of a plain duty. I do not sympathize with the sentiment that Congress in session is dangerous to our general business interests. Its members are the agents of the people, and their presence at the seat of Government in the execution of the sovereign will should not operate as an injury, but a benefit. There could be no better time to put the Government upon a sound financial and economic basis than now. The people have only recently voted that this should be done, and nothing is more binding upon the agents of their will than the obligation of immediate action. It has always seemed to me that the postponement of the meeting of Congress until more than a year after it has been chosen deprived Congress too often of the inspiration of the popular will and the country of the corresponding benefits. It is evident, therefore, that to postpone action in the presence of so great a necessity would be unwise on the part of the Executive because unjust to the interests of the people. Our action now will be freer from mere partisan consideration than if the question of tariff revision was postponed until the regular session of Congress. We are nearly two years from a Congressional election, and politics cannot so greatly distract us as if such contest was immediately pending. We can approach the problem calmly and patriotically, without fearing its effect upon an early election.

Our fellow-citizens who may disagree with us upon the character of this legislation prefer to have the question settled now, even against their preconceived views, and perhaps settled so reasonably, as I trust and believe it will be, as to insure great permanence, than to have further uncertainty menacing the vast and varied business interests of the United States. Again, whatever action Congress may take will be given a fair opportunity for trial before the people are called to pass judgment upon it, and this I consider a great essential to the rightful and lasting settlement of the question. In view of these considerations, I shall deem it my duty as President to convene Congress in extraordinary session on Monday, the 15th day of March, 1897.

In conclusion, I congratulate the country upon the fraternal spirit of the people and the manifestations of good will everywhere so apparent. The recent election not only most fortunately demonstrated the obliteration of sectional or geographical lines, but to some extent also the prejudices which for years have distracted our councils and marred our true greatness as a nation. The triumph of the people, whose verdict is carried into effect today, is not the triumph of one section, nor wholly of one party, but of all sections and all the people. The North and the South no longer divide on the old lines, but upon principles and policies; and in this fact surely every lover of the country can find cause for true felicitation. Let us rejoice in and cultivate this spirit; it is ennobling and will be both a gain and a blessing to our beloved country. It will be my constant aim to do nothing, and permit nothing to be done, that will arrest or disturb this growing sentiment of unity and co-operation, this revival of esteem and affiliation which now animates so many thousands in both the old antagonistic sections, but I shall cheerfully do everything possible to promote and increase it.

Let me again repeat the words of the oath administered by the Chief Justice which, in their respective sphere, so far as applicable, I would have all my countrymen observe: "I will faithfully execute the office of President of the United States, and will, to the best of my ability, preserve, protect, and defend the Constitution of the United States." This is the obligation I have reverently taken before the Lord Most High. To keep it will be my single purpose, my constant prayer; and I shall confidently rely upon the forbearance and assistance of all the people in the discharge of my solemn responsibilities.

SPECIAL MESSAGE

EXECUTIVE MANSION, May 17, 1897

To the Senate and House of Representatives of the United States:

Official information from our consuls in Cuba establishes the fact that a large number of American citizens in the island are in a state of destitution, suffering for want of food and medicines. This applies particularly to the rural districts of the central and eastern parts.

The agricultural classes have been forced from their farms into the nearest towns, where they are without work or money. The local authorities of the several towns, however kindly disposed, are unable to relieve the needs of their own people and are altogether powerless to help our citizens.

The latest report of Consul-General Lee estimates six to eight hundred Americans are without means of support. I have assured him that provision would be made at once to relieve them. To that end I recommend that Congress make an appropriation of not less than $50,000 to be immediately available, for use under the direction of the Secretary of State.

It is desirable that a part of the sum which may be appropriated by Congress should, in the discretion of the Secretary of State, also be used for the transportation of American citizens who, desiring to return to the United States, are without means to do so.

WILLIAM McKINLEY

McKINLEY PROMPTS THE SPANIARDS:

A DIRECTIVE FROM THE STATE DEPARTMENT
July 16, 1897

*The new President soon decided that he should continue
the line of policy that Cleveland had initiated in his ap-
peal to Spain in April, 1896. After some delay, McKinley
selected Stewart Lyndon Woodford, a former Union general
and well-known New York lawyer, to be his minister in
Madrid. He asked Woodford to stop en route to his post
for conversations with the American ambassadors to
Britain, France, and Germany. On July 16, 1897, just
before the general departed, the Secretary of State gave
him the following directive.*

Before you go to your post it is proper to state to you the President's views on the relation of your Government to the contest which
is now being waged in Cuba. The same occasion requires that you
should be made acquainted with the course which has been deemed
best for the United States to follow under existing conditions. . . .

For more than two years a wholly unexampled struggle has raged
in Cuba between the discontented native population and the mother
power. Not only has its attendant ruin spread over a larger area than
in any previous contest, but its effects have been more widely felt
and the cost of life and treasure to Spain has been far greater. The
strife continues on a footing of mutual destruction and devastation.
Day by day the conviction gathers strength that it is visionary for
Spain to hope that Cuba, even if eventually subjugated by sheer exhaustion, can ever bear to her anything like the relation of dependence
and profit she once bore. The policy which obviously attempts to
make Cuba worthless to the Cubans, should they prevail, must inevitably make the island equally worthless to Spain in the event of
reconquest, whether it be regained as a subject possession or endowed
with a reasonable measure of self-administration.

The recuperative processes, always painfully slow in an exhausted
community, would necessarily be doubly remote in either of the latter
contingencies, for in the light of events of the past twenty-nine years
capital and industry would shrink from again engaging in costly enterprises in a field where neither proximate return nor permanent
security is to be expected. To fix the truth of this assertion one need
only regard the fate of the extraordinary efforts to rehabilitate the
fortunes of Cuba that followed the truce of 1878. The capital and intel-
ligence contributed by citizens of the United States and other countries, which at that time poured into Cuba seeking to endow the island with the marvelous resources of modern invention and advanced
industrial processes, have now become submerged in the common
ruin. The commerce of Cuba has dwindled to such unprofitable proportions that its ability for self-support is questionable even if peace
was restored today. Its capacity to yield anything like adequate return

toward the support of the mother country, even granting the disposition to do so, is a matter of the gravest doubt.

Weighing all these facts carefully and without prejudice, in the judgment of the President the time has come for this Government to soberly consider and clearly decide the nature and methods of its duty both to its neighbors and itself.

This Government has labored and is still laboring under signal difficulties in its administration of its neutrality laws. It is ceaselessly confronted with questions affecting the inherent and treaty rights of its citizens in Cuba. It beholds the island suffering an almost complete paralysis of many of its most necessary commercial functions by reason of the impediments imposed and the ruinous injuries wrought by this internecine warfare at its very doors; and above all, it is naturally and rightfully apprehensive lest some untoward incident may abruptly supervene to inflame mutual passions beyond control and thus raise issues which, however deplorable, can not be avoided.

In short, it may not be reasonably asked or expected that a policy of mere inaction can be safely prolonged. There is no longer question that the sentiment of the American people strongly demands that if the attitude of neutrality is to be maintained toward these combatants it must be a genuine neutrality as between combatants, fully recognized as such in fact as well as in name. The problem of recognition of belligerency has been often presented, but never perhaps more explicitly than now. Both Houses of Congress, nearly a year ago, adopted by an almost unanimous vote a concurrent resolution recognizing belligerency in Cuba, and latterly the Senate, by a large majority, has voted a joint resolution of like purport, which is now pending in the House of Representatives.

At this juncture our Government must seriously inquire whether the time has not arrived when Spain, of her own volition, moved by her own interests and by every paramount sentiment of humanity, will put a stop to this destructive war and make proposals of settlement honorable to herself and just to her Cuban colony and to mankind. The United States stands ready to assist her and tender good offices to that end.

It should by no means be forgotten that besides and beyond the question of recognition of belligerency, with its usual proclamation of neutrality and its concession of equal rights and impartial imposition of identical disabilities in respect to the contending parties within our municipal jurisdiction, there lies the larger ulterior problem of intervention, which the President does not now discuss. It is with no unfriendly intent that this subject has been mentioned, but simply to show that this Government does not and can not ignore the possibilities of duty hidden in the future, nor be unprepared to face an emergency which may at any time be born of the unhappy contest in Cuba. The extraordinary, because direct and not merely theoretical or sentimental, interest of the United States in the Cuban situation can not be ignored, and if forced the issue must be met honestly and fearlessly, in conformity with our national life and character. Not only are our citizens largely concerned in the ownership of property and in the industrial and commercial ventures which have been set on foot in Cuba through our enterprising initiative and sustained by their capital, but the chronic condition of trouble and violent derangement in that island constantly causes disturbance in the social and political condition of our own people. It keeps up a continuous irritation within our own borders, injuriously affects the normal functions of business, and tends to delay the condition of prosperity to which this country is entitled.

No exception can be taken to the general proposition that a neighboring nation, however deeply disturbed and injured by the existence of a devastating internal conflict at its doors, may be constrained, on grounds of international comity, to disregard its endangered interests and remain a passive spectator of the contest for a reasonable time while the titular authority is repressing the disorder. The essence of this moral obligation lies in the reasonableness of the delay invited by circumstances and by the effort of the territorial authority to assert its claimed rights. The onlooking nation need only wait "a reasonable time" before alleging and acting upon the rights which it, too, possesses. This proposition is not a legal subtlety, but a broad principle of international comity and law.

The question arises, then, whether Spain has not already had a reasonable time to restore peace and been unable to do so, even by a concentration of her resources and measures of unparalleled severity which have received very general condemnation. The methods which Spain has adopted to wage the fight give no prospect of immediate peace or of a stable return to the conditions of prosperity which are essential to Cuba in its intercourse with its neighbors. Spain's inability entails upon the United States a degree of injury and suffering which can not longer be ignored. Assuredly Spain can not expect this Government to sit idle, letting vast interests suffer, our political elements disturbed, and the country perpetually embroiled, while no progress is being made in the settlement of the Cuban problem. Such a policy of inaction would in reality prove of no benefit to Spain, while certain to do the United States incalculable harm. This Government, strong in its sense of right and duty, yet keenly sympathetic with the aspirations of any neighboring community in close touch with our own civilization, is naturally desirous to avoid, in all rational ways, the precipitation of a result which would be painfully abhorrent to the American people.

For all of the reasons before stated the President feels it his duty to make the strongest possible effort to help bring about a result which shall be in conformity alike with the feelings of our people, the inherent rights of civilized man, and be of advantage both to Cuba and to Spain. Difficult as the task may seem now, it is believed that frankness, earnestness, perseverence, and a fair regard for the rights of others will eventually solve the problem.

It should be borne in mind from the start that it is far removed from the feelings of the American people and the mind of the President to propose any solution to which the slightest idea of humiliation to Spain could in any way be attached. But no possible intention or occasion to wound the just susceptibilities of the Castilian nation can be discerned in the altogether friendly suggestion that the good offices of the United States may now be lent to the advantage of Spain.

You are hereby instructed to bring these considerations as promptly as possible, but with due allowance for favorable conditions, to the attention of the Government of Her Majesty the Queen Regent, with all the impressiveness which their importance demands, and with all the earnestness which the constantly imperiled national interests of the United States justifies. You will emphasize the self-restraint which this Government has hitherto observed until endurance has ceased to be tolerable or even possible for any longer indefinite term. You will lay especial stress on the unselfish friendliness of our desires, and upon the high purpose and sincere wish of the United States to give its aid only in order that a peaceful and enduring result may be reached, just and honorable alike to Spain and to the Cuban people, and only so far as such aid may accomplish the wished-for ends. In so doing, you will not disguise the gravity of the situation, nor conceal the President's conviction that, should his present effort be fruitless, his duty to his countrymen will necessitate an early decision as to the course of action which the time and the transcendent emergency may demand.

As to the manner in which the assistance of the United States can be effectively rendered in the Cuban situation, the President has no desire to embarrass the Government of Spain by formulating precise proposals. All that is asked or expected is that some safe way may be provided for action which the United States may undertake with justice and self-respect, and that the settlement shall be a lasting one, honorable and advantageous to Spain and to Cuba and equitable to the United States.

THE ALTERNATIVES IN CUBA
December 6, 1897

*From February 1895, when the insurrection against Span-
ish rule had begun in Cuba, the American government had
tried to maintain a position of neutrality. Neither President Cleveland nor President McKinley wanted war with
Spain. But the prolongation of the rebellion led jingoists
and interventionists in this country to agitate and propo-
gandize for American involvement. McKinley, in 1897, was
heartened by a change within the Spanish government to a
more liberal ministry that pledged reform in Cuba. In the
following portion of his first annual message to Congress
on December 6, 1897, McKinley reviewed the Cuban situation and discussed possible courses of action. He demonstrated a patience that exasperated many of his fellow
Republicans; but within a few months McKinley would
reverse his stand.*

The most important proble with which this government is now
called upon to deal pertaining to its foreign relations concerns its
duty toward Spain and the Cuban insurrection. Problems and conditions more or less in common with those now existing have confronted
this government at various times in the past. The story of Cuba for
many years has been one of unrest; growing discontent; an effort
toward a larger enjoyment of liberty and self-control; of organized
resistance to the mother country; of depression after distress and
warfare and of ineffectual settlement to be followed by renewed revolt.
For no enduring period since the enfranchisement of the continental
possessions of Spain in the Western continent has the condition of
Cuba or the policy of Spain toward Cuba not caused concern to the
United States.

The prospect from time to time that the weakness of Spain's hold
upon the island and the political vicissitudes and embarrassments of
the home government might lead to the transfer of Cuba to a continental power called forth, between 1823 and 1860, various emphatic
declarations of the policy of the United States to permit no disturbance
of Cuba's connection with Spain unless in the direction of independence
or acquisition by us through purchase; nor has there been any change
of this declared policy since upon the part of the government.

The revolution which began in 1868 lasted for ten years, despite
the strenuous efforts of the successive peninsular governments to
suppress it. Then as now, the government of the United States testified
its grave concern and offered its aid to put an end to bloodshed in
Cuba. The overtures made by General Grant were refused and the
war dragged on, entailing great loss of life and treasure and increased
injury to American interests besides throwing enhanced burdens of
neutrality upon this government. In 1878, peace was brought about by

the Truce of Zanjon, obtained by negotiations between the Spanish commander, Martinez de Campos, and the insurgent leaders.

The present insurrection broke out in February 1895. It is not my purpose at this time to recall its remarkable increase or to character-ize its tenacious resistance against the enormous forces massed against it by Spain. The revolt and the efforts to subdue it carried destruction to every quarter of the island, developing wide proportions and defying the efforts of Spain for its suppression. The civilized code of war has been disregarded, no less so by the Spaniards than by the Cubans.

The existing conditions cannot but fill this government and the American people with the gravest apprehension. There is no desire on the part of our people to profit by the misfortunes of Spain. We have only the desire to see the Cubans prosperous and contented, enjoying that measure of self-control which is the inalienable right of man, protected in their right to reap the benefit of the exhaustless treasures of their country.

The offer made by my predecessor in April 1896, tendering the friendly offices of this Government, failed. Any mediation on our part was not accepted. In brief, the answer read: "There is no effectual way to pacify Cuba unless it begins with the actual submission of the rebels to their mother country." Then only could Spain act in the promised direction, of her own motion and after her own plans.

The cruel policy of concentration was initiated February 16, 1896. The productive districts controlled by the Spanish armies were de-populated. The agricultural inhabitants were herded in and about the garrison towns, their lands laid waste and their dwellings destroyed. This policy the late cabinet of Spain justified as a necessary measure of war and as a means of cutting off supplies from the insurgents. It has utterly failed as a war measure. It was not a civilized warfare. It was extermination.

Against this abuse of the rights of war I have felt constrained on repeated occasions to enter the firm and earnest protest of this Government. There was much of public condemnation of the treatment of American citizens by alleged illegal arrests and long imprisonment awaiting trial or pending protracted judicial proceedings. I felt it my first duty to make instant demand for the release or speedy trial of all American citizens under arrest. Before the change of the Spanish cabinet in October last twenty-two prisoners, citizens of the United States, had been given their freedom.

The instructions given to our new minister to Spain before his de-parture for his post directed him to impress upon that government the sincere wish of the United States to lend its aid toward the ending of the war in Cuba by reaching a peaceful and lasting result, just and honorable alike to Spain and to the Cuban people. These instructions recited the character and duration of the contest, the widespread losses it entails, the burdens and restraints it imposes upon us, with constant disturbance of national interests, and the injury resulting from an indefinite continuance of this state of things.

It was stated that at this juncture our government was constrained to seriously inquire if the time was not ripe when Spain of her own volition, moved by her own interests and every sentiment of humanity, should put a stop to this destructive war and make proposals of settlement honorable to herself and just to her Cuban colony. It was urged that as a neighboring nation, with large interests in Cuba, we could be required to wait only a reasonable time for the mother country to establish its authority and restore peace and order within the borders of the island; that we could not contemplate an indefinite period for the accomplishment of this result.

No solution was proposed to which the slightest idea of humiliation to Spain could attach, and indeed precise proposals were withheld to avoid embarrassment to that government. All that was asked or expected was that some safe way might be speedily provided and permanent peace restored. It so chanced that the consideration of this offer, addressed to the same Spanish administration, which had declined the tenders of my predecessor and which for more than two years had poured men and treasure into Cuba in the fruitless effort to suppress the revolt, fell to others. Between the departure of General Woodford, the new envoy, and his arrival in Spain the statesman who had shaped the policy of this country fell by the hand of an assassin, and although the cabinet of the late premier still held office and received from our envoy the proposals he bore, that cabinet gave place within a few days thereafter to a new administration, under the leadership of Sagasta.

The reply to our note was received on the 23rd day of October. It is in the direction of a better understanding. It appreciates the friendly purposes of this government. It admits that our country is deeply affected by the war in Cuba and that its desires for peace are just. It declares that the present Spanish government is bound by every consideration to a change of policy that should satisfy the United States and pacify Cuba within a reasonable time. To this end Spain has decided to put into effect the political reforms heretofore advocated by the present premier, without halting for any consideration in the path which in its judgment leads to peace. The military operations, it is said, will continue but will be humane and conducted with all regard for private rights, being accompanied by political action leading to the autonomy of Cuba while guarding Spanish sovereignty.

This, it is claimed, will result in investing Cuba with a distinct personality; the island to be governed by an executive and by a local council or chamber, reserving to Spain the control of the foreign relations, the army and navy, and the judicial administration. To accomplish this, the present government proposes to modify existing legislation by decree, leaving the Spanish Cortes, with the aid of Cuban senators and deputies, to solve the economic problem and properly distribute the existing debt.

In the absence of a declaration of the measures that this government proposes to take in carrying out its proffer of good offices, it suggests that Spain be left free to conduct military operations and grant political reforms, while the United States for its part shall enforce its neutral obligations and cut off the assistance which it is asserted the insurgents receive from this country. The supposition of an indefinite prolongation of the war is denied. It is asserted that the western provinces are already well-nigh reclaimed; that the planting of cane and tobacco therein has been resumed, and that by force of arms and new and ample reforms very early and complete pacification is hoped for.

The immediate amelioration of existing conditions under the new administration of Cuban affairs is predicted, and therewithal the disturbance and all occasion for any change of attitude on the part of the United States. Discussion of the question of the international duties and responsibilities of the United States as Spain understands them is presented, with an apparent disposition to charge us with failure in this regard. This charge is without any basis in fact. It could not have been made if Spain had been cognizant of the constant efforts this government has made at the cost of millions and by the employment of the administrative machinery of the nation at command to perform its full duty according to the law of nations. That it has successfully prevented the departure of a single military expedition or armed vessel from our shores in violation of our laws would seem to be a sufficient answer. But of this aspect of the Spanish note it is not necessary to speak further now. Firm in the conviction of a wholly performed obligation, due response to this charge has been made in diplomatic course.

Throughout all these horrors and dangers to our own peace this government has never in any way abrogated its sovereign prerogative of reserving to itself the determination of its policy and course according to its own high sense of right and in consonance with the dearest interests and convictions of our own people should the prolongation of the strife so demand.

Of the untried measures there remain only: recognition of the insurgents as belligerents, recognition of the independence of Cuba; neutral intervention to end the war by imposing a rational compromise between the contestants, and intervention in favor of one or the other party. I speak not of forcible annexation, for that cannot be thought of. That by our code of morality would be criminal aggression.

Recognition of the belligerency of the Cuban insurgents has often been canvassed as a possible if not inevitable step both in regard to the previous ten years' struggle and during the present war. I am not unmindful that the two houses of Congress in the spring of 1896 expressed the opinion by concurrent resolution that a condition of public war existed, requiring or justifying the recognition of a state of belligerency in Cuba; and, during the extra session, the Senate voted a joint resolution of like import, which however was not brought to a vote in the House of Representatives.

In the presence of these significant expressions of the sentiment of the legislative branch, it behooves the executive to soberly consider the conditions under which so important a measure must needs rest for justification. It is to be seriously considered whether the Cuban insurrection possesses beyond dispute the attributes of statehood, which alone can demand the recognition of belligerency in its favor. Possession, in short, of the essential qualifications of sovereignty by the insurgents and the conduct of the war by them according to the received code of war are no less important factors toward the determination of the problem of belligerency than are the influences and consequences of the struggle upon the internal policy of the recognizing state.

The wise utterances of President Grant in his memorable message of December 8, 1875, are signally relevant to the present situation in Cuba, and it may be wholesome now to recall them. At this time a ruinous conflict had for seven years wasted the neighboring island. During all those years an utter disregard of the laws of civilized warfare and of the just demands of humanity, which called forth expressions of condemnation from the nations of Christendom, continued unabated. Desolation and ruin pervaded that productive region, enormously affecting the commerce of all commercial nations, but that of the United States more than any other by reason of proximity and larger trade and intercourse. At that juncture General Grant uttered these words, which now, as then, sum up the elements of the problem:

"A recognition of the independence of Cuba being, in my opinion, impracticable and indefensible, the question which next presents itself is that of the recognition of belligerent rights in the parties to the contest.

In a former message to Congress I had occasion to consider this question, and reached the conclusion that the conflict in Cuba, dreadful and devastating as were its incidents, did not rise to the fearful dignity of war. . . . It is possible that the acts of foreign powers, and even acts of Spain herself, of this very nature, might be pointed to in defense of such recognition. But now, as in its past history, the United States should carefully avoid the false lights which might lead it into the mazes of doubtful law and of questionable propriety, and adhere rigidly and sternly to the rule, which has been its guide, of doing only that which is right and honest and of good report. The question of according or of withholding rights of belligerency must be judged in every case in view of the particular attending facts. Unless justified by necessity, it is always, and justly, regarded as an unfriendly act and a gratuitous demonstration of moral support to the rebellion. It is necessary, and it is required, when the interests and rights of another governor of its people are so far affected by a pending civil conflict as to require a definition of its relations to the parties thereto. But this conflict must be one which will be recognized in the sense of international law as war. Belligerence, too, is a fact. The mere existence of contending armed bodies and their occasional conflicts do not constitute war in the sense referred to. Applying to the existing condition of affairs in Cuba the tests recognized by publicists and writers on international law, and which have been observed by nations of dignity, honesty, and power when free from sensitive or selfish and unworthy motives, I fail to find in the insurrection the existence of such a substantial political organization, real, palpable, and manifest to the world, having the forms and capable of the ordinary functions of government toward its own people and to other states, with courts for the administration of justice, with a local habitation, possessing such organization of force, such material, such occupation of territory, as to take the contest out of the category of a mere rebellious insurrection or occasional skirmishes and place it on the terrible footing of war, to which a recognition of belligerency would aim to elevate it. The contest, moreover, is solely on land; the insurrection has not possessed itself of a single seaport whence it may send forth its flag, nor has it any means of communication with foreign powers except through the military lines of its adversaries. No apprehension of any of those sudden and difficult complications which a war upon the ocean is apt to precipitate upon the vessels, both commercial and national, and upon the consular officers of other powers calls for the definition of their relations to the parties to the contest. Considered as a question of expediency, I regard the accordance of belligerent rights still to be as unwise and premature as I regard it to be, at present, indefensible as a measure of right. Such recognition entails upon the country according the rights which flow from it difficult and complicated duties, and requires the exaction from the contending parties of the strict observance of their rights and obligations. It confers the right of search upon the high seas by vessels of both parties; it would subject the carrying of arms and munitions of war, which now may be transported freely and without interruption in the vessels of the United States, to detention and to possible seizure; it would give rise to countless vexatious questions, would release the parent Government from responsibility for acts done by the insurgents, and would invest Spain with the right to exercise the supervision recognized by our treaty of 1795 over our commerce on the high seas, a very large part of which, in its traffic between the Atlantic and the Gulf States and between all of them and the States on the Pacific, passes through the waters which wash the shores of Cuba. The exercise of this supervision could scarce fail to lead, if not to abuses, certainly to collisions perilous to the peaceful relations of the two

States. There can be little doubt as to what result such supervision would before long draw this nation. It would be unworthy of the United States to inaugurate the possibilities of such result by measures of questionable right or expediency or by any indirection.''

Turning to the practical aspects of a recognition of belligerency and reviewing its inconveniences and positive dangers, still further pertinent considerations appear. In the code of nations there is no such thing as a naked recognition of belligerency unaccompanied by the assumption of international neutrality. Such recognition without more will not confer upon either party to a domestic conflict a status not theretofore actually possessed or affect the relation of either party to other states. The act of recognition usually takes the form of a solemn proclamation of neutrality which recites the de facto condition of belligerency as 'its motive. It announces a domestic law of neutrality in the declaring state. It assumes the international obligations of a neutral in the presence of a public state of war. It warns all citizens and others within the jurisdiction of the proclaimant that they violate those rigorous obligations at their own peril and cannot expect to be shielded from the consequences. The right of visit and search on the seas and seizure of vessels and cargoes and contraband of war and good prize under admiralty law must under international law be admitted as a legitimate consequence of a proclamation of belligerency.

While according the equal belligerent rights defined by public law to each party in our ports disfavors would be imposed on both, which while nominally equal would weigh heavily in behalf of Spain herself. Possessing a navy and controlling the ports of Cuba her maritime rights could be asserted not only for the military investment of the island but up to the margin of our own territorial waters, and a condition of things would exist for which the Cubans within their own domain could not hope to create a parallel; while its creation through aid or sympathy from within our domain would be even more impossible than now, with the additional obligations of international neutrality we would perforce assume.

The enforcement of this enlarged and onerous code of neutrality would only be influential within our own jurisdiction by land and sea and applicable by our own instrumentalities. It could impart to the United States no jurisdiction between Spain and the insurgents. It would give the United States no right of intervention to enforce the conduct of the strife within the paramount authority of Spain according to the international code of war.

For these reasons I regard the recognition of the belligerency of the Cuban insurgents as now unwise and therefore inadmissible. Should that step hereafter be deemed wise as a measure of right and duty, the executive will take it.

Intervention upon humanitarian grounds has been frequently suggested and has not failed to receive my most anxious and earnest

consideration, But should such a step be now taken when it is apparent
that a hopeful change has supervened in the policy of Spain toward Cuba?
A new government has taken office in the mother country. It is pledged
in advance to the declaration that all the effort in the world cannot suffice to maintain peace in Cuba by the bayonet; that vague promises of
reform after subjugation afford no solution of the insular problem;
that with a substitution of commanders must come a change of the
past system of warfare for one in harmony with a new policy which
shall no longer aim to drive the Cubans to the "horrible alternative
of taking to the thicket or succumbing in misery"; that reforms must be
instituted in accordance with the needs and circumstances of the time,
and that these reforms, while designed to give full autonomy to the
colony and to create a virtual entity and self-controlled administration,
shall yet conserve and affirm the sovereignty of Spain by a just distribution of powers and burdens upon a basis of mutual interest un-
tainted by methods of selfish expediency.

The first acts of the new government lie in these honorable paths.
The policy of cruel rapine and extermination that so long shocked the
universal sentiment of humanity has been reversed. Under the new
military commander a broad clemency is proffered. Measures have
already been set on foot to relieve the horrors of starvation. The
power of the Spanish armies, it is asserted, is to be used not to
spread ruin and desolation but to protect the resumption of peaceful
agricultural pursuits and productive industries. That past methods
are futile to force a peace by subjugation is freely admitted, and that
ruin without conciliation must inevitably fail to win for Spain the
fidelity of a contented dependency.

Decrees in application of the foreshadowed reforms have already
been promulgated. The full text of these decrees has not been received, but as furnished in a telegraphic summary from our minister
are: All civil and electoral rights of peninsular Spaniards are, in
virtue of existing constitutional authority, forthwith extended to colonial Spaniards. A scheme of autonomy has been proclaimed by decree, to become effective upon ratification by the Cortes. It creates
a Cuban parliament which, with the insular executive, can consider
and vote upon all subjects affecting local order and interests, possessing unlimited powers, save as to matters of state, war, and the navy,
as to which the governor-general acts by his own authority as the del-
egate of the central government. This parliament receives the oath of
the governor-general to preserve faithfully the liberties and privil-
eges of the colony, and to it the colonial secretaries are responsible.
It has the right to propose to the central government, through the
governor-general, modifications of the national charter and to invite
new projects of law or executive measures in the interest of the colony.

Besides its local powers, it is competent, first, to regulate electoral registration and procedure and prescribe the qualifications of electors and the manner of exercising suffrage; second, to organize courts of justice with native judges from members of the local bar; third, to frame the insular budget both as to expenditures and revenues, without limitation of any kind, and to set apart the revenues to meet the Cuban share of the national budget, which latter will be voted by the national Cortes with the assistance of Cuban senators and deputies; fourth, to initiate or take part in the negotiations of the national government for commercial treaties which may affect Cuban interests; fifth, to accept or reject commercial treaties which the national government may have concluded without the participation of the Cuban government; sixth, to frame the colonial tariff, acting in accord with the peninsular government in scheduling articles of mutual commerce between the mother country and the colonies. Before introducing or voting upon a bill, the Cuban government or the chambers will lay the project before the central government and hear its opinion thereon, all the correspondence in such regard being made public. Finally, all conflicts of jurisdiction arising between the different municipal, provincial, and insular assemblies, or between the latter and the insular executive power, and which from their nature may not be referable to the central government for decision, shall be submitted to the courts.

That the government of Sagasta has entered upon a course from which recession with honor is impossible can hardly be questioned; that in the few weeks it has existed it has made earnest of the sincerity of its professions is undeniable. I shall not impugn its sincerity, nor should impatience be suffered to embarrass it in the task is has undertaken. It is honestly due to Spain and to our friendly relations with Spain that she should be given a reasonable chance to realize her expectations and to prove the asserted efficacy of the new order of things to which she stands irrevocably committed. She has recalled the commander whose brutal orders inflamed the American mind and shocked the civilized world. She has modified the horrible order of concentration and has undertaken to care for the helpless and permit those who desire to resume the cultivation of their fields to do so and assures them of the protection of the Spanish government in their lawful occupations. She has just released the "Competitor" prisoners heretofore sentenced to death and who have been the subject of repeated diplomatic correspondence during both this and the preceding administration.

Not a single American citizen is now in arrest or confinement in Cuba of whom this government has any knowledge. The near future will demonstrate whether the indispensable condition of a righteous peace, just alike to the Cubans and to Spain as well as equitable to all our interests so intimately involved in the welfare of Cuba, is likely to be attained. If not, the exigency of further and other action by the United States will remain to be taken. When that time comes that action will be determined in the line of indisputable right and duty. It will be faced, without misgiving or hesitancy, in the light of the obligation this government owes to itself, to the people who have confided to it the protection of their interests and honor, and to humanity.

Sure of the right, keeping free from all offense ourselves, actuated only by upright and patriotic considerations, moved neither by passion nor selfishness, the government will continue its watchful care over the rights and property of American citizens and will abate none of its efforts to bring about by peaceful agencies a peace which shall be honorable and enduring. If it shall hereafter appear to be a duty imposed by our obligations to ourselves, to civilization and humanity, to intervene with force, it shall be without fault on our part and only because the necessity for such action will be so clear as to command the support and approval of the civilized world.

WILLIAM McKINLEY

AMERICAN ULTIMATUM TO SPAIN

After McKinley's message to Congress in December 1897, the Cuban situation worsened rather than improved. The American battleship Maine *was blown up in Havana Harbor on February 15, 1898, and the newspapers that had been urging war with Spain for the past year stepped up their campaign. The slogan of the hour was: "Remember the* Maine, *to hell with Spain!" In this fiery atmosphere, the State Department sent a series of cablegrams to Stewart L. Woodford, the U.S. ambassador to Spain, stating the American position regarding Cuba. Two messages sent during the last week in March are reprinted here.*

March 26, 1898

The President's desire is for peace. He cannot look upon the suffering and starvation in Cuba save with horror. The concentration of men, women, and children in the fortified towns and permitting them to starve is unbearable to a Christian nation geographically so close as ours to Cuba. All this has shocked and inflamed the American mind, as it has the civilized world, where its extent and character are known.

It was represented to him in November that the Blanco government would at once release the suffering and so modify the Weyler order as to permit those who were able to return to their homes and till the fields from which they had been driven. There has been no relief to the starving except such as the American people have supplied. The reconcentration order has not been practically superseded.

There is no hope of peace through Spanish arms. The Spanish government seems unable to conquer the insurgents. More than half of the island is under control of the insurgents. For more than three years our people have been patient and forbearing; we have patrolled our coast with zeal and at great expense, and have successfully prevented the landing of any armed force on the island. The war has disturbed the peace and tranquility of our people.

We do not want the island. The President has evidenced in every way his desire to preserve and continue friendly relations with Spain. He has kept every international obligation with fidelity. He wants an honorable peace. He has repeatedly urged the government of Spain to secure such a peace. She still has the opportunity to do it, and the President appeals to her from every consideration of justice and humanity to do it. Will she? Peace is the desired end.

For your own guidance, the President suggests that if Spain will revoke the reconcentration order and maintain the people until they can support themselves and offer to the Cubans full self-government, with reasonable indemnity, the President will gladly assist in its consummation. If Spain should invite the United States to mediate for peace and the insurgents would make like request, the President might undertake such office of friendship.

March 27, 1898

Believed the Maine report will be held in Congress for a short time without action. A feeling of deliberation prevails in both houses of Congress. See if the following can be done:

First, armistice until October 1. Negotiations meantime looking for peace between Spain and insurgents through friendly offices of President United States.

Second, immediate revocation of reconcentrado order so as to permit people to return to their farms and the needy to be relieved with provisions and supplies from United States cooperating with authorities so as to afford full relief.

Add, if possible, third, if terms of peace not satisfactorily settled by October 1, President of the United States to be final arbiter between Spain and insurgents.

If Spain agrees, President will use friendly offices to get insurgents to accept plan. Prompt action desirable.

SPECIAL MESSAGE

EXECUTIVE MANSION, March 28, 1898

To the Congress of the United States:

For some time prior to the visit of the <u>Maine</u> to Havana Harbor our consular representatives pointed out the advantages to flow from the visit of national ships to the Cuban waters, in accustoming the people to the presence of our flag as the symbol of good will and of our ships in the fulfillment of the mission of protection to American interests, even though no immediate need therefor might exist.

Accordingly, on the 24th of January last, after conference with the Spanish minister, in which the renewal of visits of our war vessels to Spanish waters was discussed and accepted, the peninsular authorities at Madrid and Havana were advised of the purpose of this Government to resume friendly naval visits at Cuban ports, and that in that view the <u>Maine</u> would forthwith call at the port of Havana.

This announcement was received by the Spanish Government with appreciation of the friendly character of the visit of the <u>Maine</u> and with notification of intention to return the courtesy by sending Spanish ships to the principal ports of the United States. Meanwhile the <u>Maine</u> entered the port of Havana on the 25th of January, her arrival being marked with no special incident besides the exchange of customary salutes and ceremonial visits.

The <u>Maine</u> continued in the harbor of Havana during the three weeks following her arrival. No appreciable excitement attended her stay. On the contrary, a feeling of relief and confidence followed the resumption of the long-interrupted friendly intercourse. So noticeable was this immediate effect of her visit that the consul-general strongly urged that the presence of our ships in Cuban waters should be kept up by retaining the <u>Maine</u> at Havana, or, in the event of her recall, by sending another vessel there to take her place.

At forty minutes past 9 in the evening of the 15th of February the <u>Maine</u> was destroyed by an explosion, by which the entire forward part of the ship was utterly wrecked. In this catastrophe 2 officers and 264 of her crew perished, those who were not killed outright by her explosion being penned between decks by the tangle of wreckage and drowned by the immediate sinking of the hull.

Prompt assistance was rendered by the neighboring vessels anchored in the harbor, aid being especially given by the boats of the Spanish cruiser <u>Alfonso</u> XII and the Ward Line steamer <u>City of Washington</u>, which lay not far distant. The wounded were generously cared for by the authorities of Havana, the hospitals being freely opened to them, while the earliest recovered bodies of the dead were interred by the municipality in a public cemetery in the city. Tributes of grief and sympathy were offered from all official quarters of the island.

The appalling calamity fell upon the people of our country with crushing force, and for a brief time an intense excitement prevailed, which in a community less just and self-controlled than ours might have led to hasty acts of blind resentment. This spirit, however, soon gave way to the calmer processes of reason and to the resolve to investigate the facts and await material proof before forming a judgment as to the cause, the responsibility, and, if the facts warranted, the remedy due. This course necessarily recommended itself from the outset to the Executive, for only in the light of a dispassionately ascertained certainty could it determine the nature and measure of its full duty in the matter.

The usual procedure was followed, as in all cases of casualty or disaster to national vessels of any maritime state. A naval court of inquiry was at once organized, composed of officers well qualified by rank and practical experience to discharge the onerous duty imposed upon them. Aided by a strong force of wreckers and divers, the court proceeded to make a thorough investigation on the spot, employing every available means for the impartial and exact determination of the causes of the explosion. Its operations have been conducted with the utmost deliberation and judgment, and, while independently pursued, no attainable source of information was neglected, and the fullest opportunity was allowed for a simultaneous investigation by the Spanish authorities.

The finding of the court of inquiry was reached, after twenty-three days of continuous labor, on the 21st of March instant, and, having been approved on the 22d by the commander in chief of the United States naval force on the North Atlantic station, was transmitted to the Executive.

It is herewith laid before the Congress, together with the voluminous testimony taken before the court.

Its purport is, in brief, as follows:

When the Maine arrived at Havana, she was conducted by the regular Government pilot to buoy No. 4, to which she was moored in from 5 1/2 to 6 fathoms of water.

The state of discipline on board and the condition of her magazines, boilers, coal bunkers, and storage compartments are passed in review, with the conclusion that excellent order prevailed and that no indication of any cause for an internal explosion in any quarter.

At 8 o'clock in the evening of February 15 everything had been reported secure, and all was quiet.

At forty minutes past 9 o'clock the vessel was suddenly destroyed.

There were two distinct explosions, with a brief interval between them. The first lifted the forward part of the ship very perceptibly;

the second, which was more open, prolonged, and of greater volume, is attributed by the court to the partial explosion of two or more of the forward magazines.

The evidence of the divers established that the after part of the ship was practically intact and sank in that condition a very few moments after the explosion. The forward part was completely demolished.

Upon the evidence of a concurrent external cause the finding of the court is as follows:

At frame 17 the outer shell of the ship, from a point 11 1/2 feet from the middle line of the ship and 6 feet above the keel when in its normal position, has been forced up so as to be now about 4 feet above the surface of the water, therefore about 34 feet above where it would be had the ship sunk uninjured.

The outside bottom plating bent into a reversed V shape (A), the after wing of which, about 15 feet broad and 32 feet in length (from frame 17 to frame 25), is doubled back upon itself against the continuation of the same plating, extending forward.

At frame 18 the vertical keel is broken in two and the flat keel bent into an angle similar to the angle formed by the outside bottom plates. This break is now about 6 feet below the surface of the water and about 30 feet above its normal position.

In the opinion of the court this effect could have been produced only by the explosion of a mine situated under the bottom of the ship at about frame 18 and somewhat on the port side of the ship.

The conclusions of the court are:

The loss of the Maine was not in any respect due to fault or negligence on the part of any of the officers or members of her crew;

That the ship was destroyed by the explosion of a submarine mine, which caused the partial explosion of two or more of her forward magazines; and

That no evidence has been obtainable fixing the responsibility for the destruction of the Maine upon any person or persons.

I have directed that the finding of the court of inquiry and the views of this Government thereon be communicated to the Government of Her Majesty the Queen Regent, and I do not permit myself to doubt that the sense of justice of the Spanish nation will dictate a course of action suggested by honor and the friendly relations of the two Governments.

It will be the duty of the Executive to advise the Congress of the result, and in the meantime deliberate consideration is invoked.

WILLIAM McKINLEY

WAR MESSAGE OR PEACE PROBE?
April 11, 1898

*The Spanish government sincerely wished to avoid war
with the United States. But it faced tremendous internal
problems coupled with a military situation in Cuba that
had gotten out of control. In an effort to appease the
Americans without provoking the wrath of opposition
groups at home, it agreed to two of the main conditions
that the United States had laid down as necessary to gain
peace in Cuba: the governor-general of Cuba was instructed by Spain to revoke reconcentration (a brutal policy of
committing Cubans to camps); and the commander of the
Spanish Army, on April 9, was told to grant an armistice
to the insurgents as a prelude to peace. Although McKinley knew of these concessions, he went before Congress
on April 11 to request the use of military and naval forces
of the United States in order to secure "a full and final
termination of hostilities between the government of Spain
and the people of Cuba." Passages from this message are
reprinted below. It did not close the door to a negotiated
settlement and is so worded.*

Obedient to that precept of the Constitution which commands the
President to give from time to time to the Congress information of
the state of the Union and to recommend to their consideration such
measures as he shall judge necessary and expedient, it becomes my
duty now to address your body with regard to the grave crisis that has
arisen in the relations of the United States to Spain by reason of the
warfare that for more than three years has raged in the neighboring
island of Cuba.

I do so because of the intimate connection of the Cuban question
with the state of our own Union and the grave relation the course which
it is now incumbent upon the nation to adopt must needs bear to the
traditional policy of our government if it is to accord with the precepts
laid down by the founders of the republic and religiously observed by
succeeding administrations to the present day.

The present revolution is but the successor of other similar in-
surrections which have occurred in Cuba against the dominion of
Spain, extending over a period of nearly half a century, each of which,
during its progress, has subjected the United States to great effort
and expense in enforcing its neutrality laws, caused enormous losses
to American trade and commerce, caused irritation, annoyance, and
disturbance among our citizens, and, by the exercise of cruel, bar-
barous, and uncivilized practices of warfare, shocked the sensibilities
and offended the humane sympathies of our people.

Since the present revolution began in February 1895, this country has seen the fertile domain at our threshold ravaged by fire and sword, in the course of a struggle unequaled in the history of the island and rarely paralleled as to the numbers of the combatants and the bitterness of the contest by any revolution of modern times, where a dependent people striving to be free have been opposed by the power of the sovereign state.

Our people have beheld a once prosperous community reduced to comparative want, its lucrative commerce virtually paralyzed, its exceptional productiveness diminished, its fields laid waste, its mills in ruins, and its people perishing by tens of thousands from hunger and destitution. We have found ourselves constrained, in the observance of that strict neutrality which our laws enjoin, and which the law of nations commands, to police our own waters and watch our own seaports in prevention of any unlawful act in aid of the Cubans.

Our trade has suffered, the capital invested by our citizens in Cuba has been largely lost, and the temper and forbearance of our people have been so sorely tried as to beget a perilous unrest among our own citizens, which has inevitably found its expression from time to time in the national legislature; so that issues wholly external to our own body politic engross attention and stand in the way of that close devotion to domestic advancement that becomes a self-contained commonwealth, whose primal maxim has been the avoidance of all foreign entanglements. All this must needs awaken, and has, indeed, aroused the utmost concern on the part of this government, as well during my predecessor's term as in my own.

In April 1896, the evils from which our country suffered through the Cuban war became so onerous that my predecessor made an effort to bring about a peace through the mediation of this government in any way that might tend to an honorable adjustment of the contest between Spain and her revolted colony, on the basis of some effective scheme of self-government for Cuba under the flag and sovereignty of Spain. It failed through the refusal of the Spanish government then in power to consider any form of mediation or, indeed, any plan of settlement which did not begin with the actual submission of the insurgents to the mother country, and then only on such terms as Spain herself might see fit to grant. The war continued unabated. The resistance of the insurgents was in nowise diminished. . . .

By the time the present administration took office a year ago, reconcentration — so called — had been made effective over the better part of the four central and western provinces — Santa Clara, Matanzas, Habana, and Pinar del Rio. . . .

In this state of affairs, my administration found itself confronted with the grave problem of its duty. My message of last December reviewed the situation and narrated the steps taken with a view to relieving its acuteness and opening the way to some form of honorable settlement. The assassination of the prime minister, Canovas, led to a change of government in Spain. The former administration, pledged to subjugation without concession, gave place to that of a more liberal party, committed long in advance to a policy of reform, involving the wider principle of home rule for Cuba and Puerto Rico. . . .

The war in Cuba is of such a nature that short of subjugation or extermination a final military victory for either side seems impracticable. The alternative lies in the physical exhaustion of the one or the other party, or perhaps of both – a condition which in effect ended the ten years' war by the truce of Zanjon. The prospect of such a protraction and conclusion of the present strife is a contingency hardly to be contemplated with equanimity by the civilized world, and least of all by the United States, affected and injured as we are, deeply and intimately, by its very existence.

Realizing this, it appeared to be my duty, in a spirit of true friendliness, no less to Spain than to the Cubans who have so much to lose by the prolongation of the struggle, to seek to bring about an immediate termination of the war. To this end I submitted, on the 27th ultimo, as a result of much representation and correspondence, through the United States minister at Madrid, propositions to the Spanish government looking to an armistice until October 1 for the negotiation of peace with the good offices of the President.

In addition, I asked the immediate revocation of the order of reconcentration, so as to permit the people to return to their farms and the needy to be relieved with provisions and supplies from the United States, cooperating with the Spanish authorities, so as to afford full relief.

The reply of the Spanish cabinet was received on the night of the 31st ultimo. It offered, as the means to bring about peace in Cuba, to confide the preparation thereof to the insular parliament, inasmuch as the concurrence of that body would be necessary to reach a final result, it being, however, understood that the powers reserved by the constitution to the central government are not lessened or diminished. As the Cuban parliament does not meet until the 4th of May next, the Spanish government would not object, for its part, to accept at once a suspension of hostilities if asked for by the insurgents from the general in chief, to whom it would pertain, in such case, to determine the duration and conditions of the armistice.

The propositions submitted by General Woodford and the reply of the Spanish government were both in the form of brief memoranda, the texts of which are before me, and are substantially in the language above given. The function of the Cuban parliament in the matter of "preparing" peace and the manner of its doing so are not expressed in the Spanish memorandum; but from General Woodford's explanatory reports of preliminary discussions preceding the final conference it is understood that the Spanish government stands ready to give the insular congress full powers to settle the terms of peace with the insurgents, whether by direct negotiation or indirectly by means of legislation does not appear.

With this last overture in the direction of immediate peace, and its disappointing reception by Spain, the Executive is brought to the end of his effort.

In my annual message of December last I said:

"Of the untried measures there remained only: Recognition of the insurgents as belligerents; recognition of the independence of Cuba; neutral intervention to end the war by imposing a rational compromise between the contestants, and intervention in favor of one or the other party. I speak not of forcible annexation, for that cannot be thought of. That, by our code of morality, would be criminal aggression."

Thereupon I reviewed these alternatives, in the light of President Grant's measured words, uttered in 1875, when, after seven years of sanguinary, destructive, and cruel hostilities in Cuba, he reached the conclusion that the recognition of the independence of Cuba was impracticable and indefensible, and that the recognition of belligerence was not warranted by the facts according to the tests of public law. I commented especially upon the latter aspect of the question, pointing out the inconveniences and positive dangers of a recognition of belligerence which, while adding to the already onerous burdens of neutrality within our own jurisdiciton, could not in any way extend our influence or effective offices in the territory of hostilities.

Nothing has since occurred to change my view in this regard, and I recognize as fully now as then that the issuance of a proclamation of neutrality, by which process the so-called recognition of belligerents is published, could, of itself and unattended by other action, accomplish nothing toward the one end for which we labor – the instant pacification of Cuba and the cessation of the misery that afflicts the island.

I said in my message of December last: "It is to be seriously considered whether the Cuban insurrection possesses beyond dispute the attributes of statehood which alone can demand the recognition of belligerency in its favor." The same requirement must certainly be no less seriously considered when the graver issue of recognizing independence is in question, for no less positive test can be applied to the greater act than to the lesser; while, on the other hand, the influences and consequences of the struggle upon the internal policy of the recognizing state, which form important factors when the recognition of belligerency is concerned, are secondary, if not rightly eliminable, factors when the real question is whether the community claiming recognition is or is not independent beyond peradventure.

Nor from the standpoint of expediency do I think it would be wise or prudent for this government to recognize at the present time the independence of the so-called Cuban Republic. Such recognition is not necessary in order to enable the United States to intervene and pacify the island. To commit this country now to the recognition of any particular government in Cuba might subject us to embarrassing conditions of international obligation toward the organization so recognized. In case of intervention our conduct would be subject to the approval or disapproval of such government. We would be required to submit to its direction and to assume to it the mere relation of a friendly ally.

When it shall appear hereafter that there is within the island a government capable of performing the duties and discharging the functions of a separate nation, and having, as a matter of fact, the proper forms and attributes of nationality, such government can be promptly and readily recognized and the relations and interests of the United States with such nation adjusted.

There remain the alternative forms of intervention to end the war, either as an impartial neutral by imposing a rational compromise between the contestants, or as the active ally of the one party or the other.

As to the first, it is not to be forgotten that during the last few months the relation of the United States has virtually been one of friendly intervention in many ways, each not of itself conclusive, but all tending to the exertion of a potential influence toward an ultimate pacific result, just and honorable to all interests concerned. The spirit of all our acts hitherto has been an earnest, unselfish desire for peace and prosperity in Cuba, untarnished by difference between us and Spain, and unstained by the blood of American citizens.

The forcible intervention of the United States as a neutral to stop the war, according to the large dictates of humanity and following many historical precedents where neighboring states have interfered to check the hopeless sacrifices of life by internecine conflicts beyond their borders, is justifiable on rational grounds. It involves, however, hostile constraint upon both the parties to the contest as well to enforce a truce as to guide the eventual settlement.

The grounds for such intervention may be briefly summarized as follows:

First, in the cause of humanity and to put an end to the barbarities, bloodshed, starvation, and horrible miseries now existing there, and which the parties to the conflict are either unable or unwilling to stop or mitigate. It is no answer to say this is all in another country, belonging to another nation, and is therefore none of our business. It is specially our duty, for it is right at our door.

Second, we owe it to our citizens in Cuba to afford them that protection and indemnity for life and property which no government there can or will afford, and to that end to terminate the conditions that deprive them of legal protection.

Third, the right to intervene may be justified by the very serious injury to the commerce, trade, and business of our people and by the wanton destruction of property and devastation of the island.

Fourth, and which is of the utmost importance, the present condition of affairs in Cuba is a constant menace to our peace, and entails upon this government an enormous expense. With such a conflict waged for years in an island so near us and with which our people have such trade and business relations; when the lives and liberty of our citizens are in constant danger and their property destroyed and themselves ruined; where our trading vessels are liable to seizure and are seized at our very door by warships of a foreign nation, the expeditions of filibustering that we are powerless to prevent altogether, and the irritating questions and entanglements thus arising — all these and others that I need not mention, with the resulting strained relations, are a constant menace to our peace, and compel us to keep on a semiwar footing with a nation with which we are at peace.

These elements of danger and disorder already pointed out have been strikingly illustrated by a tragic event which has deeply and justly moved the American people. I have already transmitted to Congress the report of the Naval Court of Inquiry on the destruction of the battleship Maine in the harbor of Havana during the night of the 15th of February. The destruction of that noble vessel has filled the national heart with inexpressible horror. Two hundred and fifty-eight brave sailors and marines and two officers of our Navy, reposing in the fancied security of a friendly harbor, have been hurled to death, grief and want brought to their homes, and sorrow to the nation.

The Naval Court of Inquiry, which, it is needless to say, commands the unqualified confidence of the government, was unanimous in its conclusions that the destruction of the Maine was caused by an exterior explosion, that of a submarine mine. It did not assume to place the resonsibility. That remains to be fixed.

In any event, the destruction of the Maine by whatever exterior cause, is a patent and impressive proof of a state of things in Cuba that is intolerable. That condition is thus shown to be such that the Spanish government cannot assure safety and security to a vessel of the American Navy in the harbor of Havana on a mission of peace, and rightfully there. . . .

The long trial has proved that the object for which Spain has waged the war cannot be attained. The fire of insurrection may flame or may smolder with varying seasons, but it has not been, and it is plain that it cannot be, extinguished by present methods. The only hope of relief and repose from a condition which can no longer be endured is the enforced pacification of Cuba. In the name of humanity, in the name of civilization, in behalf of endangered American interests which gave us the right and the duty to speak and to act, the war in Cuba must stop.

In view of these facts and of these considerations, I ask the Congress to authorize and empower the President to take measures to secure a full and final termination of hostilities between the government of Spain and the people of Cuba, and to secure in the island the establishment of a stable government, capable of maintaining order and observing its international obligations, insuring peace and tranquility and the security of its citizens as well as our own, and to use the military and naval forces of the United States as may be necessary for these purposes.

And in the interest of humanity and to aid in preserving the lives of the starving people of the island, I recommend that the distribution of food and supplies be continued, and that an appropriation be made out of the public Treasury to supplement the charity of our citizens.

The issue is now with the Congress. It is a solemn responsibility. I have exhausted every effort to relieve the intolerable condition of affairs which is at our doors. Prepared to execute every obligation imposed upon me by the Constitution and the law, I await your action.

Yesterday, and since the preparation of the foregoing message, official information was received by me that the latest decree of the queen regent of Spain directs General Blanco, in order to prepare and facilitate peace, to proclaim a suspension of hostilities, the duration and details of which have not yet been communicated to me.

This fact with every other pertinent consideration will, I am sure, have your just and careful attention in the solemn deliberations upon which you are about to enter. If this measure attains a successful result, then our aspirations as a Christian, peace-loving people will be realized. If it fails, it will be only another justification for our contemplated action.

WILLIAM McKINLEY

THE INDEPENDENCE OF CUBA
April 20, 1898

April 11, McKinley sent his message to Congress recom-
mending intervention in Cuba. The Joint Resolution of
April 20 authorized the use of the army and the navy to
effect Cuban independence; the formal declaration of war
followed April 25. The most important of the resolutions
of April 20 was the fourth, known as the Teller Amend-
ment.

Joint resolution for the recognition of the independence of the people of Cuba, demanding that the Government of Spain relinquish its authority and government in the Island of Cuba, and to withdraw its land and naval forces from Cuba and Cuban waters, and directing the President of the United States to use the land and naval forces of the United States to carry these resolutions into effect.

Whereas the abhorrent conditions which have existed for more than three years in the Island of Cuba, so near our own borders, have shocked the moral sense of the people of the United States, have been a disgrace to Christian civilization, culminating, as they have, in the destruction of a United States battle ship, with two hundred and sixty-six of its officers and crew, while on a friendly visit in the harbor of Havana, and can not longer be endured, as has been set forth by the President of the United States in his message to Congress of April eleventh, eighteen hundred and ninety-eight, upon which the action of Congress was invited, Therefore,

Resolved, First. That the people of the Island of Cuba are, and of right ought to be, free and independent.

Second. That it is the duty of the United States to demand, and the Government of the United States does hereby demand that the Government of Spain at once relinquish its authority and government in the Island of Cuba and withdraw its land and naval forces from Cuba and Cuban waters.

Third. That the President of the United States be, and he hereby is, directed and empowered to use the entire land and naval forces of the United States and to call into the actual service of the United States the militia of the several States, to such extent as may be necessary to carry these resolutions into effect.

Fourth. That the United States hereby disclaims any disposition or intention to exercise sovereignty, jurisdiction, or control over said Island except for the pacification thereof, and asserts its determination, when that is accomplished, to leave the government and control of the Island to its people.

THE ANNEXATION OF HAWAII
July 7, 1898

Though President Cleveland withdrew from the Senate the Treaty of 1893 providing for the annexation of the Hawaiian Islands and denounced the methods by which the Hawaiian revolution had been brought about, Queen Liliuokalani was not restored to the throne. In July 1894 the Republic of Hawaii was established, and was recognized by the United States. Agitation for annexation continued, and a second treaty of annexation was concluded in 1897. While this treaty was still pending in the Senate the war with Spain broke out and the United States used the islands as a naval base. The islands were then annexed by joint resolution in order to avoid the danger of rejection by a third of the Senate. During the flood of congressional oratory, President McKinley threatened to annex the Hawaiian Islands by executive decree as a war measure. Finally the House of Representatives passed the resolution of June 15, the Senate on July 6. President McKinley affixed his signature the following day, July 7. This annexation pleased sea power enthusiast Admiral Alfred T. Mahan and others who regarded Hawaii as the key that unlocked the Pacific.

Whereas the Government of the Republic of Hawaii having, in due form, signified its consent, in the manner provided by its constitution, to cede absolutely and without reserve to the United States of America all rights of sovereignty of whatever kind in and over the Hawaiian Islands and their dependencies, and also to cede and transfer to the United States the absolute fee and ownership of all public, Government, or Crown lands, public buildings or edifices, ports, harbors, military equipment, and all other property of every kind and description belonging to the Government of the Hawaiian Islands together with every right and appurtenance thereunto appertaining. Therefore,

Resolved by the Senate and the House of Representatives of the United States of America in Congress assembled. That said cession is accepted, ratified, and confirmed, and that the said Hawaiian Islands and their dependencies be, and they are hereby, annexed as part of the territory of the United States and are subject to the sovereign dominion thereof, and that all and singular the property and rights hereinbefore mentioned are vested in the United States of America.

The existing laws of the United States relative to public lands shall not apply to such lands in the Hawaiian Islands; but the Congress of the United States shall enact special laws for their management and disposition: Provided, That all revenue from or proceeds of the same, except as regards such parts thereof as may be used or occupied for the civil, military, or naval purposes of the United States, or may be assigned for the use of the local government, shall be used solely for the benefit of the inhabitants of the Hawaiian Islands for educational and other public purposes.

Until Congress shall provide for the government of such islands all the civil, judicial and military powers exercised by the officers of the existing government in said islands shall be vested in such person or persons and shall be exercised in such a manner as the President of the United States shall direct; and the President shall have the power to remove said officers and fill the vacancies so occasioned.

The existing treaties of the Hawaiian Islands with foreign nations shall forthwith cease and determine, being replaced by such treaties as may exist, or as may be hereafter concluded, between the United States and such foreign nations. The municipal legislation of the Hawaiian Islands, not enacted for the fulfillment of the treaties so extinguished, and not inconsistent with this joint resolution nor contrary to the Constitution of the United States nor to any existing treaty of the United States, shall remain in force until the Congress of the United States shall otherwise determine.

Until such legislation shall be enacted extending the United States customs laws and regulations to the Hawaiian Islands the existing customs relations of the Hawaiian Islands with the United States and other countries shall remain unchanged.

The public debt of the Republic of Hawaii, lawfully existing at the date of the passage of this joint resolution, including the amounts due to depositors in the Hawaiian Postal Savings Bank, is hereby assumed by the Government of the United States; but the liability of the United States in this regard shall in no case exceed four million dollars. So long, however, as the existing Government and the present commercial relations of the Hawaiian Islands are continued as hereinbefore provided said Government shall continue to pay the interest on said debt.

There shall be no further immigration of Chinese into the Hawaiian Islands, except upon such conditions as are now or may hereafter be allowed by the laws of the United States; and no Chinese, by reason of anything herein contained, shall be allowed to enter the United States from the Hawaiian Islands.

The President shall appoint five commissioners, at least two of whom shall be residents of the Hawaiian Islands, who shall, as soon as practicable, recommend to Congress such legislation concerning the Hawaiian Islands as they shall deem necessary or proper. . . .

THE TASTE OF EMPIRE
September 16, 1898

*One of the most articulate spokesman for American im-
perialism was Albert Beveridge of Indiana. While cam-
paigning for the Senate, he perfected the oratorical style
that came to characterize his arguments for empire build-
ing during his years on Capitol Hill. Beveridge's position
was simple enough: he believed that the Americans were
the chosen people, that our form of government was the
best in the world and should therefore be exported to other
countries, and that it was not only to our commercial and
political but also to our moral advantage to expand beyond our borders. In a campaign speech, given in Indian-
apolis on September 16, 1898, and reprinted here in part,
Beveridge explained why the United States should keep
the Philippine Islands.*

It is a noble land that God has given us; a land that can feed and
clothe the world; a land whose coastlines would enclose half the countries of Europe; a land set like a sentinel between the two imperial
oceans of the globe; a greater England with a nobler destiny. It is a
mighty people that He has planted on this soil; a people sprung from
the most masterful blood of history; a people perpetually revitalized
by the virile, man-producing working folk of all the earth; a people
imperial by virtue of their power, by right of their institutions, by
authority of their heaven-directed purposes — the propogandists and
not the misers of liberty.

It is a glorious history our God has bestowed upon His chosen
people; a history whose keynote was struck by Liberty Bell; a history
heroic with faith in our mission and our future; a history of statesmen
who flung the boundaries of the republic out into unexplored lands and
savage wildernesses; a history of soldiers who carried the flag across
the blazing deserts and through the ranks of hostile mountains, even
to the gates of sunset; a history of a multiplying people who overran
a continent in half a century; a history of prophets who saw the consequences of evils inherited from the past and of martyrs who died to
save us from them; a history divinely logical, in the process of whose
tremendous reasoning we find ourselves today.

Therefore, in this campaign, the question is larger than a party
question. It is an American question. It is a world question. Shall the
American people continue their resistless march toward the commercial supremacy of the world? Shall free institutions broaden their
blessed reign as the children of liberty wax in strength, until the empire of our principles is established over the hearts of all mankind?

Have we no mission to perform, no duty to discharge to our fellow-
man? Has the Almighty Father endowed us with gifts beyond our des-

erts and marked us as the people of His peculiar favor, merely to
rot in our own selfishness, as men and nations must who take cow-
ardice for their companions and self for their deity – as China has, as
India has, as Egypt has?

Shall we be as the man who had one talent and hid it, or as he who
had ten talents and used them until they grew to riches? And shall we
reap the reward that waits on our discharge of our high duty as the
sovereign power of earth; shall we occupy new markets for what our
farmers raise, new markets for what our factories make, new markets
for what our merchants sell – aye, and, please God, new markets for
what our ships shall carry?

Shall we avail ourselves of new sources of supply of what we do not
raise or make so that what are luxuries today will be necessities tomorrow? Shall our commerce be encouraged until, with Oceanica,
the Orient, and the world, American trade shall be the imperial trade of
the entire globe? Shall we conduct the mightiest commerce of history
with the best money known to man, or shall we use the pauper money
of Mexico, of China, and of the Chicago platform?

What are the great facts of this administration? Not a failure of
revenue; not a perpetual battle between the executive and legislative
departments of government; not a rescue from dishonor by European
syndicates at the price of tens of millions in cash and national humiliation unspeakable. These have not marked the past two years – the
past two years, which have blossomed into four splendid months of
glory.

But a war has marked it, the most holy ever waged by one nation
against another – a war for civilization, a war for a permanent peace,
a war which, under God, although we knew it not, swung open to the
republic the portals of the commerce of the world. And the first
question you must answer with your vote is whether you endorse that
war. We are told that all citizens and every platform endorse the war,
and I admit, with the joy of patriotism, that this is true. But that is
only among ourselves, and we are of and to ourselves no longer.

This election takes place on the stage of the world, with all earth's
nations for our auditors. If the administration is defeated at the polls,
will England believe that we accept the results of the war? Will Germany, that sleepless searcher for new markets for her factories and
fields, and therefore the effective meddler in all international complications – will Germany be discouraged from interfering with our
settlement of the war if the administration is defeated at the polls?
Will Russia, that weaver of the webs of commerce into which province
after province and people after people falls, regard us as a steadfast
people if the administration is defeated at the polls?

The world is observing us today. Not a foreign office in Europe
that is not studying the American republic and watching the American

elections of 1898 as it never watched an American election before. Are the American people the chameleon of the nations? "If so, we can easily handle them," say the diplomats of the world. . . .

The world still rubs its eyes from its awakening to the resistless power and sure destiny of this republic. Which outcome of this election will be best for America's future, which will most healthfully impress every people of the globe with the steadfastness of character and tenacity of purpose of the American people – the triumph of the government at the polls or the success of the opposition?

I repeat, it is more than a party question. It is an American question. It is an issue in which history sleeps. It is a situation which will influence the destiny of the republic. . . .

God bless the soldiers of 1898, children of the heroes of 1861, descendants of the heroes of 1776! In the halls of history they will stand side by side with those elder sons of glory, and the opposition to the government at Washington shall not deny them. No! They shall not be robbed of the honor due them, nor shall the republic be robbed of what they won for their country. For William McKinley is continuing the policy that Jefferson began, Monroe continued, Seward advanced, Grant promoted, Harrison championed, and the growth of the republic has demanded.

Hawaii is ours; Puerto Rico is to be ours; at the prayer of the people, Cuba will finally be ours; in the islands of the East, even to the gates of Asia, coaling stations are to be ours; at the very least the flag of a liberal government is to float over the Philippines, and I pray God it may be the banner that Taylor unfurled in Texas and Frémont carried to the coast – the stars and stripes of glory.

And the burning question of this campaign is whether the American people will accept the gifts of events; whether they will rise as lifts their soaring destiny; whether they will proceed upon the lines of national development surveyed by the statesmen of our past; or whether, for the first time, the American people doubt their mission, question fate, prove apostate to the spirit of their race, and halt the ceaseless march of free institutions.

The opposition tells us that we ought not to govern a people without their consent. I answer: The rule of liberty, that all just government derives its authority from the consent of the governed, applies only to those who are capable of self-government. . . .

They ask us how we will govern these new possessions. I answer: Out of local conditions and the necessities of the case methods of government will grow. If England can govern foreign lands, so can America. If Germany can govern foreign lands, so can America. If they can supervise protectorates, so can America. Why is it more difficult to administer Hawaii than New Mexico or California? Both had a savage and an alien population; both were more remote from the seat of government when they came under our dominion than Hawaii is today.

Will you say by your vote that American ability to govern has decayed; that a century's experience in self-rule has failed of a result? Will you affirm by your vote that you are an infidel to American vigor and power and practical sense; or that we are of the ruling race of the world, that ours is the blood of government, ours the heart of dominion, ours the brain and genius of administration? Will you remember that we do but what our fathers did — we but pitch the tents of liberty farther westward, farther southward — we only continue the march of the flag.

The march of the flag! . . .

Distance and oceans are no arguments. The fact that all the territory our fathers bought and seized is contiguous is no argument. In 1819, Florida was farther from New York than Puerto Rico is from Chicago today; Texas, farther from Washington in 1845 than Hawaii is from Boston in 1898; California, more inaccessible in 1847 than the Philippines are now. Gibraltar is farther from London than Havana is from Washington; Melbourne is farther from Liverpool than Manila is from San Francisco. The ocean does not separate us from lands of our duty and desire — the oceans join us, a river never to be dredged, a canal never to be repaired.

Steam joins us; electricity joins us — the very elements are in league with our destiny. Cuba not contiguous! Puerto Rico not contiguous! Hawaii and the Philippines not contiguous! Our Navy will make them contiguous. Dewey and Sampson and Schley have made them contiguous, and American speed, American guns, American heart and brain and nerve will keep them contiguous forever.

But the opposition is right — there is a difference. We did not need the western Mississippi Valley when we acquired it, nor Florida, nor Texas, nor California, nor the royal provinces of the far Northwest. We had no emigrants to people this imperial wilderness, no money to develop it, even no highways to cover it. No trade awaited us in its savage fastnesses. Our productions were not greater than our trade. There was not one reason for the landlust of our statesmen from Jefferson to Grant, other than the prophet and the Saxon within them.

But today we are raising more than we can consume. Today we are making more than we can use. Today our industrial society is congested; there are more workers than there is work; there is more capital than there is investment. We do not need more money — we need more circulation, more employment. Therefore we must find new markets for our produce, new occupation for our capital, new work for our labor. And so, while we did not need the territory taken during the past century at the time it was acquired, we do need what we have taken in 1898, and we need it now.

Think of the thousands of Americans who will pour into Hawaii and Puerto Rico when the republic's laws cover those islands with justice and safety! Think of the tens of thousands of Americans who will invade mine and field and forest in the Philippines when a liberal government, protected and controlled by this republic, if not the government of the republic itself, shall establish order and equity there! Think of the hundreds of thousands of Americans who will build a soap-and-water, common-school civilization of energy and industry in Cuba when a government of law replaces the double reign of anarchy and tyranny. Think of the prosperous millions that empress of islands will support when, obedient to the law of political gravitation, her people ask for the highest honor liberty can bestow, the sacred Order of the Stars and Stripes, the citizenship of the Great Republic!

What does all this mean for every one of us? It means opportunity for all the glorious young manhood of the republic — the most virile, ambitious, impatient, militant manhood the world has ever seen. It means that the resources and the commerce of these immensely rich dominions will be increased as much as American energy is greater than Spanish sloth; for Americans henceforth will monopolize those resources and that commerce. . . .

It means new employment and better wages for every laboring man in the Union. It means higher prices for every bushel of wheat and corn, for every pound of butter and meat, for every item that the farmers of this republic produce. It means active, vigorous, constructive investment of every dollar of moldy and miserly capital in the land.

It means all this tomorrow, and all this forever, because it means not only the trade of the prize provinces but the beginning of the commercial empire of the republic. . . . I said, the commercial empire of the republic. That is the greatest fact of the future. And that is why these islands involve considerations larger than their own commerce. The commercial supremacy of the republic means that this nation is to be the sovereign factor in the peace of the world. For the conflicts of the future are to be conflicts of trade — struggles for markets — commercial wars for existence. And the golden rule of peace is impregnability of position and invincibility of preparation. . . .

Ah! as our commerce spreads, the flag of liberty will circle the globe and the highways of the ocean — carrying trade to all mankind — be guarded by the guns of the republic. And as their thunders salute the flag, benighted peoples will know that the voice of liberty is speaking, at last, for them; that civilization is dawning, at last, for them — liberty and civilization, those children of Christ's gospel, who follow and never precede the preparing march of commerce.

It is the tide of God's great purposes made manifest in the instincts of our race, whose present phase is our personal profit, but whose far-off end is the redemption of the world and the Christianization of mankind. And he who throws himself before that current is like him who, with puny arm, tries to turn the Gulf Stream from its course, or stay, by idle incantations, the blessed processes of the sun.

Shall this future of the race be left with those who, under God, began this career of sacred duty and immortal glory; or shall we risk it to those who would scuttle the ship of progress and build a dam in the current of destiny's large designs?. . .

There are so many real things to be done — canals to be dug, railways to be laid, forests to be felled, cities to be built, unviolated fields to be tilled, priceless markets to be won, ships to be launched, peoples to be saved, civilization to be proclaimed, and the flag of liberty flung to the eager air of every sea. Is this an hour to waste upon triflers with nature's laws? Is this a season to give our destiny over to wordmongers and prosperity wreckers? Is this a day to think of office seekers, to be cajoled by the politician's smile, or seduced by the handshake of hypocrisy? No! No! my fellow citizens!

It is an hour to remember your duty to the home. It is a moment to realize the opportunities fate has opened to this favored people and to you. It is a time to bethink you of the conquering march of the flag. It is a time to bethink you of your nation and its sovereignty of the seas. It is a time to remember that the God of our fathers is our God, and that the gifts and the duties He gave to them, enriched and multiplied, He renews to us, their children.

And so it is an hour for us to stand by the government at Washington, now confronting the enemy in diplomacy, as our loyal hearts on land and sea stood to their guns and stood by the flag when they faced the enemy in war. It is a time to strengthen and sustain that devoted man, servant of the people and of the most high God, who patiently, silently, safely is guiding the republic out into the ocean of world interests and possibilities infinite. It is a time to cheer the beloved President of God's chosen people, till the whole world is vocal with American loyalty to the American government.

Fellow Americans, we are God's chosen people. Yonder at Bunker Hill and Yorktown His providence was above us. At New Orleans and on ensanguined seas His hand sustained us. Abraham Lincoln was His minister, and His was the Altar of Freedom the boys in blue set on a hundred battlefields. His power directed Dewey in the East, and delivered the Spanish Fleet into our hands on the eve of Liberty's natal day, as He delivered the elder Armada into the hands of our English sires two centuries ago. His great purposes are revealed in the progress of the flag, which surpasses the intentions of congresses and cabinets, and leads us like a holier pillar of cloud by day and pillar of fire by night into situations unforeseen by finite wisdom and duties unexpected by the unprophetic heart of selfishness.

The American people cannot use a dishonest medium of exchange; it is ours to set the world its example of right and honor. We cannot fly from our world duties; it is ours to execute the purpose of a fate that has driven us to be greater than our small intentions. We cannot retreat from any soil where Providence has unfurled our banner; it is ours to save that soil for liberty and civilization. For liberty and civilization and God's promise fulfilled, the flag must henceforth be the symbol and the sign to mankind — the flag!

ALBERT J. BEVERIDGE

WILLIAM McKINLEY AND THE
PHILIPPINE PROBLEM (1899)

When the United States entered the Spanish-American War, there were very few demands for American acquisition of the Philippine Islands. The average American had little knowledge of their existence. President McKinley and most of his Administration had entertained no thought of obtaining additional territory as the fruits of the war. Far from having designs on the Philippines, McKinley was reported to have had only a vague idea of their location when informed of Admiral Dewey's victory at Manila. It was not long, however, before the victories of American arms prepared the way for a colonial career for the United States. The bulk of the nation's press began declaring for expansion on military, religious, commercial, and humanitarian grounds. American businessmen who had previously opposed the war underwent a conversion and began to talk of the Philippines as a gateway to the markets of eastern Asia. The Protestant clergy became convinced that expansion could pay dividends in the salvation of human souls. The servant of his party rather than its leader, McKinley eventually became an expansionist as the tide of imperialism made such a course safe and practical. Below, McKinley relates how he arrived at the decision to annex the Philippines. It is significant that considerations of national interest played little part in his thinking. Moreover, he appeared unconcerned with the difficulty of defending the islands. But in the long run, the islands were to be a diplomatic and military liability to American policies in the Pacific. One scholar has even stated that "the acquisition of the Philippines was the greatest blunder of American diplomacy."

I have been criticized a good deal about the Philippines, but don't deserve it. The truth is I didn't want the Philippines, and when they came to us, as a gift from the gods, I did not know what to do with them. When the Spanish War broke out, Dewey was at Hongkong, and I ordered him to go to Manila and to capture or destroy the Spanish fleet, and he had to; because, if defeated, he had no place to refit on that side of the globe, and if the Dons were victorious, they would likely cross the Pacific and ravage our Oregon and California coasts. And so he had to destroy the Spanish fleet, and did it! But that was as far as I thought then.

When next I realized that the Philippines had dropped into our laps I confess I did not know what to do with them. I sought counsel from all sides — Democrats as well as Republicans — but got little help. I thought first we would take only Manila; then Luzon; then other islands, perhaps, also. I walked the floor of the White House night after night until midnight; and I am not ashamed to tell you, gentlemen, that I

went down on my knees and prayed Almighty God for light and guidance more than one night. And one night late it came to me this way —
I don't know how it was, but it came: (1) That we could not give them
back to Spain — that would be cowardly and dishonorable; (2) that we
could not turn them over to France, or Germany — our commercial
rivals in the Orient — that would be bad business and discreditable;
(3) that we could not leave them to themselves — they were unfit for
self-government — and they would soon have anarchy and misrule over
there worse than Spain's was; and (4) that there was nothing left for
us to do but to take them all, and to educate the Filipinos, and uplift
and civilize and Christianize them, and by God's grace do the very
best we could by them, as our fellow-men for whom Christ also died.
And then I went to bed, and went to sleep, and slept soundly, and the
next morning I sent for the chief engineer of the War Deparmtnet
(our map-maker), and I told him to put the Philippines on the map of
the United States [pointing to a large map on the wall of his office],
and there they are, and there they will stay while I am President!

SECOND INAUGURAL ADDRESS
March 4, 1901

My Fellow-Citizens:

When we assembled here on the 4th of March, 1897, there was great anxiety with regard to our currency and credit. None exists now. Then our Treasury receipts were inadequate to meet the current obligations of the Government. Now they are sufficient for all public needs, and we have a surplus instead of a deficit. Then I felt constrained to convene the Congress in extraordinary session to devise revenues to pay the ordinary expenses of the Government. Now I have the satisfaction to announce that the Congress just closed has reduced taxation in the sum of $41,000,000. Then there was deep solicitude because of the long depression in our manufacturing, mining, agricultural, and mercantile industries and the consequent distress of our laboring population. Now every avenue of production is crowded with activity, labor is well employed, and American products find good markets at home and abroad.

Our diversified productions, however, are increasing in such unprecedented volume as to admonish us of the necessity of still further enlarging our foreign markets by broader commercial relations. For this purpose reciprocal trade arrangements with other nations should in liberal spirit be carefully cultivated and promoted.

The national verdict of 1896 has for the most part been executed. Whatever remains unfulfilled is a continuing obligation resting with undiminished force upon the Executive and the Congress. But fortunate as our condition is, its permanence can only be assured by sound business methods and strict economy in national administration and legislation. We should not permit our great prosperity to lead us to reckless ventures in business or profligacy in public expenditures. While the Congress determines the objects and the sum of appropriations, the officials of the executive departments are responsible for honest and faithful disbursement, and it should be their constant care to avoid waste and extravagance.

Honesty, capacity, and industry are nowhere more indispensable than in public employment. These should be fundamental requisites to original appointment and the surest guaranties against removal.

Four years ago we stood on the brink of war without the people knowing it and without any preparation or effort at preparation for the impending peril. I did all that in honor could be done to avert the war, but without avail. It became inevitable; and the Congress at its first regular session, without party division, provided money in anticipation of the crisis and in preparation to meet it. It came. The result was signally favorable to American arms and in the highest degree honorable to the Government. It imposed upon us obligations from which we cannot escape and from which it would be dishonorable to seek escape. We are now at peace with the world, and it is my fervent prayer that if differences arise between us and other powers they may be settled by peaceful arbitration and that hereafter we may be spared the horrors of war.

Intrusted by the people for a second time with the office of President, I enter upon its administration appreciating the great responsibilities which attach to this renewed honor and commission, promising unreserved devotion on my part to their faithful discharge and reverently invoking for my guidance the direction and favor of Almighty God. I should shrink from the duties this day assumed if I did not feel that in their performance I should have the co-operation of the wise and patriotic men of all parties. It encourages me for the great task which I now undertake to believe that those who voluntarily committed to me the trust imposed upon the Chief Executive of the Republic will give to me generous support in my duties to "preserve, protect, and defend, the Constitution of the United States" and to "care that the laws be faithfully executed." The national purpose is indicated through a national election. It is the constitutional method of ascertaining the public will. When once it is registered it is a law to us all, and faithful observance should follow its decrees.

Strong hearts and helpful hands are needed, and, fortunately, we have them in every part of our beloved country. We are reunited. Sectionalism has disappeared. Division on public questions can no longer be traced by the war maps of 1861. These old differences less and less disturb the judgment. Existing problems demand the thought and quicken the conscience of the country, and the responsibility for their presence, as well as for their righteous settlement, rests upon us all — no more upon me than upon you. There are some national questions in the solution of which patriotism should exclude partisanship. Magnifying their difficulties will not take them off our hands nor facilitate their adjustment. Distrust of the capacity, integrity, and high purposes of the American people will not be an inspiring theme for future political contests. Dark pictures and gloomy forebodings are worse than useless. These only becloud, they do not help to point the way of safety and honor. "Hope maketh not ashamed." The prophets of evil were not the builders of the Republic, nor in its crises since have they saved or served it. The faith of the fathers was a mighty force in its creation, and the faith of their descendants has wrought its progress and furnished its defenders. They are obstructionists who despair, and who would destroy confidence in the ability of our people to solve wisely and for civilization the mighty problems resting upon them. The American people, intrenched in freedom at home, take their love for it with them wherever they go, and they reject as mistaken and unworthy the doctrine that we lose our own liberties by securing the enduring foundations of liberty to others. Our institutions will not deteriorate by extension, and our sense of justice will not abate under tropic suns in distant seas. As heretofore, so hereafter will the nation demonstrate its fitness to administer any new estate which events devolve upon it, and in the fear of God will "take occasion by the hand and make the bounds of freedom wider yet." If there are those among us who would make our way more difficult, we must not be disheartened, but the more earnestly dedicate ourselves to the task upon which we have rightly entered. The path of progress is seldom smooth. New things are often found hard to do. Our fathers found them so. We find them so. They are inconvenient. They cost us something. But are we not made better for the effort and sacrifice, and are not those we serve lifted up and blessed?

We will be consoled, too, with the fact that opposition has confronted every onward movement of the Republic from its opening hour until now, but without success. The Republic has marched on and on, and its step has exalted freedom and humanity. We are undergoing the same ordeal as did our predeccessors nearly a century ago. We are following the course they blazed. They triumphed. Will their successors falter and plead organic impotency in the nation? Surely after 125 years of achievement for mankind we will not now surrender our equality with other powers on matters fundamental and essential to nationality. With no such purpose was the nation created. In no such spirit has it developed its full and independent sovereignty. We adhere to the principle of equality among ourselves, and by no act of ours will we assign to ourselves a subordinate rank in the family of nations.

My fellow-citizens, the public events of the past four years have gone into history. They are too near to justify recital. Some of them were unforeseen; many of them momentous and far-reaching in their consequences to ourselves and our relations with the rest of the world. The part which the United States bore so honorably in the thrilling scenes in China, while new to American life, has been in harmony with its true spirit and best traditions, and in dealing with the results its policy will be that of moderation and fairness.

We face at this moment a most important question — that of the future relations of the United States and Cuba. With our near neighbors we must remain close friends. The declaration of the purposes of this Government in the resolution of April 20, 1898, must be made good. Ever since the evacuation of the island by the army of Spain, the Executive, with all practicable speed, has been assisting its people in the successive steps necessary to the establishment of a free and independent government prepared to assume and perform the obligations of international law which now rest upon the United States under the treaty of Paris. The convention elected by the people to frame a constitution is approaching the completion of its labors. The transfer of American control to the new government is of such great importance, involving an obligation resulting from our intervention and the treaty of peace, that I am glad to be advised by the recent act of Congress of the policy which the legislative branch of the Government deems essential to the best interests of Cuba and the United States. The principles which led to our intervention require that the fundamental law upon which the new government rests should be adapted to secure a government capable of performing the duties and discharging the functions of a separate nation, of observing its international obligations of protecting life and property, insuring order, safety, and liberty, and conforming to the established and historical policy of the United States in its relation to Cuba.

The peace which we are pledged to leave to the Cuban people must carry with it the guaranties of permanence. We became sponsors for the pacification of the island, and we remain accountable to the Cubans, no less than to our own country and people, for the reconstruction of Cuba as a free commonwealth on abiding foundations of right, justice, liberty, and assured order. Our enfranchisement of the people will not be completed until free Cuba shall "be a reality, not a name; a perfect entity, not a hasty experiment bearing within itself the elements of failure."

While the treaty of peace with Spain was ratified on the 6th of February, 1899, and ratifications were exchanged nearly two years ago, the Congress has indicated no form of government for the Philippine Islands. It has, however, provided an army to enable the Executive to suppress insurrection, restore peace, give security to the inhabitants, and establish the authority of the United States throughout the archipelago. It has authorized the organization of native troops as auxiliary to the regular force. It has been advised from time to time of the acts of the military and naval officers in the islands, of my action in appointing civil commissions, of the instructions with which they were charged, of their duties and powers, of their recommendations, and of their several acts under executive commission, together with the very complete general information they have submitted. These reports fully set forth the conditions, past and present, in the islands, and the instructions clearly show the principles which will guide the Executive until the Congress shall, as it is required to do by the treaty, determine "the civil rights and political status of the native inhabitants." The Congress having added the sanction of its authority to the powers already possessed and exercised by the Executive under the Constitution, thereby leaving with the Executive the responsibility for the government of the Philippines, I shall continue the efforts already begun until order shall be restored throughout the islands, and as fast as conditions permit will establish local governments, in the formation of which the full co-operation of the people has been already invited, and when established will encourage the people to administer them. The settled purpose, long ago proclaimed, to afford the inhabitants of the islands self-government as fast as they were ready for it will be pursued with earnestness and fidelity. Already something has been accomplished in this direction. The Government's representatives, civil and military, are doing faithful and noble work in their mission of emancipation and merit the approval and support of their countrymen. The most liberal terms of amnesty have already been communicated to the insurgents, and the way is still open for those who have raised their arms against the Government for honorable submission to its authority. Our countrymen should not be deceived. We are not waging war against the inhabitants of the Philippine Islands. A portion of them are making war against the United States. By far the greater part of the inhabitants recognize American sovereignty and welcome it as a guaranty of order and of security for life, property, liberty, freedom of conscience, and the pursuit of happiness. To them full protection will be given. They shall not be abandoned. We will not leave the destiny of the loyal millions in the islands to the disloyal thousands who are in rebellion against the United States. Order under civil institutions will come as soon as those who now break the peace shall keep it. Force will not be needed or used when those who make war against us shall make it no more. May it end without further bloodshed, and there be ushered in the reign of peace to be made permanent by a government of liberty under law!

THE PERIOD OF EXCLUSIVENESS IS PAST
September 5, 1901

This document, bearing the date of September 5, 1901, the day before McKinley was shot, is included for two reasons: 1) it serves as a last will and testament of an assassinated Chief Executive; 2) it reflects the revised views of the eminent protective tariff protagionist.

As a member of Congress McKinley's tariff views were unequivocal. In 1888, speaking in Boston, he said:

> *"I would secure the American market to the American producer, and I would not hesitate to raise the duties wherever necessary to secure this patriotic end. I would not have an idle man or an idle mill or an idle spindle in this country if, by holding exclusively the American market, we could keep them employed and running. Every yard of cloth imported here makes a demand for one yard less of American fabrication. Let England take care of herself. Let France look after her own interests. Let Germany take care of her own people; but in God's name let America look after America."*

In 1890, while chairman of the House Ways and Means Committee, McKinley sponsored the famous protective tariff legislation that bears his name. It was the highest tariff in the nation's history and the protest against such a schedule of duties helped to defeat him in a bid to keep his congressional post.

During his governorship of Ohio and ensuing hard times nationally, McKinley sought mediation between capital and labor. Invariably he manifested a good will toward the poor that was not shared by all defenders of the laissez faire system of free enterprise.

Following the Spanish-American War and President McKinley's triumphant re-election in 1900, the now popular Chief Executive made a nationwide tour from Alabama to California. Never was he more secure in the esteem of his fellow Americans, as he prepared to visit the Pan American Exposition in Buffalo, in the fall of 1901. The day before assassin Leon Czolgosz shot him, the President, speaking positively and effectively, unveiled a new way for a more international minded America.

President Milburn, Director General Buchanan, Commissioners, Ladies and Gentlemen:

I am glad to be again in the city of Buffalo and exchange greetings with her people, to whose generous hospitality I am not a stranger and with whose good will I have been repeatedly and signally honored. To-day I have additional satisfaction in meeting and giving welcome to the foreign representatives assembled here, whose presence and partici-pation in this exposition have contributed in so marked a degree to its interest and success. ... Expositions are the timekeepers of progress. They record the world's advancement. They stimulate the energy, enterprise and intellect of the people and quicken human genius. They go into the home. They broaden and brighten the daily life of the people. They open mighty storehouses of information to the student. Every expo-sition, great or small, has helped to some onward step. Comparison of ideas is always educational, and as such instruct the brain and hand of man. Friendly rivalry follows, which is the spur to industrial im-provement, the inspiration to useful invention and to high endeavor in all departments of human activity. . . .

Business life, whether among ourselves or with other people, is ever a sharp struggle for success. It will be none the less so in the future. Without competition we would be clinging to the clumsy antiquated processes of farming and manufacture and the methods of business of long ago, and the twentieth would be no further advanced than the eigh-teenth century. But though commercial competitors we are, commer-cial enemies we must not be.

The Pan-American exposition has done its work thoroughly, pre-senting in its exhibits evidences of the highest skill and illustrating the progress of the human family in the western hemisphere. This portion of the earth has no cause for humiliation for the part it has performed in the march of civilization. It has not accomplished every-thing from it. It has simply done its best, and without vanity or boast-fulness, and recognizing the manifold achievements of others, it in-vites the friendly rivalry of all the powers in the peaceful pursuits of trade and commerce, and will cooperate with all in advancing the highest and best interests of humanity. . . .

After all, how near one to the other is every part of the world. Modern inventions have brought into close relation widely separated peoples and made them better acquainted. Geographic and political divisions will continue to exist, but distances have been effaced. Swift ships and swift trains are becoming cosmopolitan. They invade fields which a few years ago were impenetrable. The world's products are exchanged as never before, and with increasing transportation facili-ties come increasing knowledge and larger trade. Prices are fixed with mathematical precision by supply and demand.The world's sell-ing prices are regulated by market and crop reports. . . .

We reached General Miles in Puerto Rico by cable, and he was able, through the military telegraph, to stop his army on the firing line with the message that the United States and Spain had signed a protocol suspending hostilities. We knew almost instantly of the first shots fired at Santiago, and the subsequent surrender of the Spanish forces was known at Washington within less than an hour of its consummation. . . .

So accustomed are we to safe and easy communication with distant lands that its temporary interruption, even in ordinary times, results in loss and inconvenience. We shall never forget the days of anxious waiting and awful suspense when no information was permitted to be sent from Pekin, and the diplomatic representatives of the nations in China, cut off from all communication, inside and outside of the walled capital, were surrounded by an angry and misguided mob that threatened their lives; nor the joy that filled the world when a single message from the Government of the United States brought through our minister the first news of the safety of the besieged diplomats. . . .

God and man have linked the nation together. No nation can longer be indifferent to any other. And as we are brought more and more in touch with each other the less occasion there is for misunderstandings and the stronger the disposition, when we have differences, to adjust them in the court of arbitration, which is the noblest forum for the settlement of international disputes.

My fellow citizens, trade statistics indicate that this country is in a state of unexampled prosperity. The figures are almost appalling. They show that we are utilizing our fields and forests and mines and that we are furnishing profitable employment to the millions of workingmen throughout the United States, bringing comfort and happiness to their homes and making it possible to lay by savings for old age and disability. That all the people are participating in this great prosperity is seen in every American community, and shown by the enormous and unprecedented deposits in our savings banks. Our duty is the care and security of these deposits, and their safe investment demands the highest integrity and the best business capacity of those in charge of these depositories of the people's earnings. . . .

By sensible trade arrangements which will not interrupt our home production we shall extend the outlets for our increasing surplus. A system which provides a mutual exchange of commodities, a mutual exchange is manifestly essential to the continued and healthful growth of our export trade. We must not repose in fancied security that we can forever sell everything and buy little or nothing. If such a thing were possible, it would not be best for us or for those with whom we deal. We should take from our customers such of their products as we can use without harm to our industries and labor. Reciprocity is the natural outgrowth of our wonderful industrial development under the domestic policy now firmly established. What we produce beyond our domestic consumption must have a vent abroad. The excess must be relieved through a foreign outlet and we should sell everywhere we can, and buy wherever the buying will enlarge our sales and productions, and thereby make a greater demand for home labor.

The period of exclusiveness is past. The expansion of our trade and commerce is the pressing problem. Commercial wars are unprofitable. A policy of good will and friendly trade relations will prevent reprisals. Reciprocity treaties are in harmony with the spirit of the times, measures of retaliation are not. If perchance some of our tariffs are no longer needed, for revenue or to encourage and protect our industries at home, why should they not be employed to extend and promote our markets abroad?

Then, too, we have inadequate steamship service. New lines of steamers have already been put in commission between the Pacific Coast ports of the United States and those on the western coasts of Mexico and Central and South America. These should be followed up with direct steamship lines between the Eastern coast of the United States and South American ports. One of the needs of the times is to direct commercial lines from our vast fields of production to the fields of consumption that we have but barely touched.

Next in advantage to having the thing to sell is to have the convenience to carry it to the buyer. We must encourage our Merchant Marine. We must have more ships. They must be under the American flag, built and manned and owned by Americans. These will not only be profitable in a commercial sense; they will be messengers of peace and amity wherever they go. We must build the Isthmian canal, which will unite the two oceans and give a straight line of water communication with the western coasts of Central and South America and Mexico. The construction of a Pacific cable cannot be longer postponed.

In the furthering of these objects of national interest and concern you are performing an important part. This exposition would have touched the heart of that American statesman whose mind was ever alert and thought ever constant for a larger commerce and a truer fraternity of the republics of the new world. His broad American spirit is felt and manifested here. He needs no identification to an assemblage of Americans anywhere, for the name of Blaine is inseparably associated with the Pan-American congress that assembles this autumn in the capital of Mexico. The good work will go on. It cannot be stopped. These buildings will disappear; this creation of art and beauty and industry will perish from sight, but their influence will remain to

> Make it live beyond its too short living
> with praises and thanksgiving. . . .

Our earnest prayer is that God will graciously vouchsafe prosperity, happiness and peace to all our neighbors, and like blessings to all the peoples and powers of earth.

BIBLIOGRAPHICAL AIDS

BIBLIOGRAPHICAL AIDS

The emphasis in this section, following the earlier volumes of the Presidential Chronologies series, is on the administration years but includes critical notations that may serve to a better understanding of the President both before and after the White House.

Additional titles can be found in "Notes and References" compiled by Margaret Leech and by H. Wayne Morgan (see Biographies below). Most students have access to Reader's Guide to Periodical Literature, Social Science and Humanities Index, and Writings in American History.

Chronological information for the period may be supplemented on two levels. Secondary students can easily consult the Encyclopedia of American History, edited by Richard B. Morris, revised edition (New York, 1965). College history majors and graduate students will find both the content and bibliography of the Harvard Guide to American History and the American Historical Association's Guide to Historical Literature indispensable aids. The Annals of America, Volume 12, dealing with Populism, Imperialism and Reform (1895-1904) can be used profitably by high school and college students.

SOURCE MATERIALS

To date there is no printed edition of William McKinley papers. In 1963 the microfilm of the McKinley Papers became available, as did the Index to the William McKinley Papers (The Library of Congress, Presidents' Papers Index Series, 481 pages). This Index, available as paperback from the Government Printing Office, Washington, D.C., covers the 98 microfilm reels (representing the McKinley holdings in the Library of Congress). William McKinley letters in other manuscript collections in the Library of Congress or elsewhere are not indexed in this volume.

The microfilm reproduction (98 reels) is of some 105,832 manuscripts and represents by far the largest known collection of McKinley papers. They were presented to the Library of Congress in 1935 by George B. Cortelyou, once a stenographer to President Grover Cleveland and later secretary to McKinley. Between 1909 and 1935 the McKinley papers were at the disposal of Charles S. Olcott, author of the official biography, The Life of William McKinley, which was published in two volumes in 1916.

Readers and researchers are referred to the "Introduction" of the Index. It features a serviceable "Provenance" and offers practical guidelines for the use of the microfilm that is available on inter-library loan from the Library of Congress and other large city, state, and university libraries. At present some 30 libraries in 19 states hold a complete or virtually complete set of McKinley papers on micro-film. Also full sets as well as individual reels are available for pur-chase by institutions and private citizens.

The location of other McKinley manuscripts is furnished in the Index, pp. v, vi and the reader is also referred to the National Catalog of Manuscript Collections and to Philip M. Hamer, A Guide to Archives and Manuscripts in the United States (1961).

For William McKinley's messages, proclamations and Executive Orders relating to the Spanish American War, see A Compilation of the Messages and Papers of the Presidents, 1789-1897, Volume 10 (J.D. Richardson, compiler, 1899), Appendix, 123-223.

BIOGRAPHIES

Leech, Margaret, In the Days of McKinley. New York, 1959. A com-prehensive study which extensively details the events of the Spanish American War and its aftermath. The author begins with McKinley as Governor of Ohio and gives a balanced view of his presidency. The study also treats sympathetically of McKinley the man and his relationship with his chronically-ill wife. Some scholars regard this biography as the first sign of a major sym-pathetic revisionism though they criticize the author's attempt at psychological description.

Morgan, H. Wayne. William McKinley and His America. Syracuse, 1963. Considered generally as the only full-length biography of the twenty-fifth president, this book strongly emphasizes the campaign of 1896 and the establishment of the McKinley Adminis-tration. Considerable stress is placed on McKinley's character as President and political leader.

Olcott, Charles Summer. The Life of William McKinley. New York, 1916, 2 vols. This work leans heavily on the notes of Mr. Geroge B. Cortelyou, Secretary to the President, as McKinley did not have an extensive correspondence. There is extensive background material for the student unfamiliar with the period.

Spielman, William Carl. William McKinley: Stalwart Republican. New York, 1954. A sketchy biographical treatment which purports to have made use of all the new material which has been revealed since Olcott's two volume work was published. It suffers from poor editing and proofreading.

ESSAYS

The student interested in the leadership qualities of William McKinley will be greatly rewarded by reading Paul S. Holbo, "Presidential Leadership in Foreign Affairs: William McKinley and the Turpie-Foraker Amendment," The American Historical Review (July, 1967). While admitting that the quality of McKinley's leadership is a highly disputed historical question, Professor Holbo attributes the anti-McKinley criticism by most historians to two factors. Partly "because Americans have varied and deeply emotional attitudes towards those men who were Presidents during wars and partly because the small, sometimes pathetic, sometimes comic Spanish American War provides such delightful examples for special pleading from history." The stereotype of McKinley as a weak President with the backbone of a "chocolate eclair" Holbo contends has no substantial basis in fact and does McKinley an injustice.

H. Wayne Morgan effectively analyzes "William McKinley as a Political Leader," in Review of Politics (October, 1966) and this essay should be read in conjunction with the same author's America's Road to Empire: The War With Spain and Overseas Expansion (New York, 1965), a persuasive pro-McKinley interpretation.

Critics of McKinley's day attacked him for not pursuing a more aggressive policy toward Spain. Later critics often condemn him for failing to restrain warlike American Opinion. Some contemporaries, however, regarded his message to Congress as both temperate and honest. See Robert J. Collier, "The President's Message," Collier's Weekly (April 23, 1898).

A splendid brief essay, replete with excellent illustrations, that depicts McKinley as a transitional Chief Executive is the account by Frank Freidel, "The American Giant Comes of Age," National Geographic (May, 1965), pp. 708-711.

MONOGRAPHS AND RELATED AREAS

Dawes, Charles G. A Journal of the McKinley Years. ed. with a foreword by Bascom N. Timmins. Chicago, 1950. The contents of the diary kept by Dawes, the Comptroller of the Currency early in the

McKinley Administration. His treatment of McKinley is concerned basically with his administration, with many personal anecdotes as the Dawes' were frequent visitors at the White House.

Filler, Louis. The President Speaks: From William McKinley to Lyndon B. Johnson. New York, 1964. The editor's introduction, entitled "The President as Symbol and as Substance," contains four useful divisions 1) "Mr. President." 2) Who They Are, 3) Power and Purpose, 4) The Voice of the Party, The Voice of the People. Only five pages are devoted to McKinley.

Freidel, Frank. The Splendid Little War. Boston, 1958, is a pictorial treatment whose text is regarded by Ernest May as "by far the best shorthand treatment."

Grenville, John A.S. and Young, George Berkeley. Politics, Strategy and American Diplomacy: Studies in Foreign Policy 1873-1917. New Haven, 1966, is a refreshingly perceptive analysis that is solidly based on newly discovered archival material in Great Britain and the United States.

Kennan, George. American Diplomacy, 1900-1950. New York, 1952*, articulately maintains that McKinley bungled the diplomatic negotiations with Spain.

LaFeber, Walter. The New Empire: An Interpretation of American Expansion, 1860-1898. Ithaca, 1963*. A study of expansionism leading up to the Spanish-American War with a heavy emphasis on economic aspects and the role of the businessman. The influence of public opinion and the sensationalist press are discounted in favor of the commercial agitation for material rewards.

Leopold, Richard W. The Growth of American Foreign Policy, New York, 1962, makes an effective case for President McKinley.

May, Ernest. Imperial Democracy: The Emergence of America as a Great Power. New York, 1961. This work offers a detailed study of the diplomacy of the period and attitudes of the European powers to the actions of the United States in the years leading up to the Spanish-American War. The author does not feel that McKinley was a very strong personality and that his dependence on the businessman made war inevitable.

May, Ernest (ed.). The Ultimate Decision: The President as Commander in Chief, New York, 1960, details McKinley's role as manager of military affairs as reflected in domestic politics.

Millis, Walter. The Martial Spirit, New York, 1931, is a literary account of the war now partially replaced by the account of Margaret Leech, In the Days of McKinley (see Biographies).

Morgan, H. Wayne. America's Road to Empire: The War with Spain and Overseas Expansion, New York, 1965, appears less defensive in tone than the author's effort (see Biographies) in 1963. Scholars find this volume more persuasive. See also Morgan's keen analysis of "William McKinley as a Political Leader," Review of Politics (October, 1966).

Pratt, Julius W. Expansionists of 1898:The Acquisition of Hawaii and the Spanish Islands, Chicago, 1964*. Originally published in 1936, this paper edition remains the most effective exposition of the role of public opinion, the yellow press, the jingoes, and the expansionists.

Van Alstyne, Richard W. The Rising American Empire, Chicago, 1965*, a provocative analysis of the origins and emergence of the United States as a national state and of its subsequent growth patterns. Chapter VII, entitled "The Thrust Into the Caribbean, 1848-1917," is recommended.

Weinberg, Albert K. Manifest Destiny: A Study of Nationalist Expansion in American History. Chicago, 1963*. This comprehensive study of the manifest destiny movement demonstrates how the expansionist philosophy is applicable to the actions of the United States in the period the Spanish-American War.

THE PRESIDENCY

Bailey, Thomas A. Presidential Greatness: The Image and the Man from George Washington to the Present. New York. 1966*. This well known author in the field of American history and biography lists more than forty yardsticks to measure presidential ability. Subjective and critical this text tests White House character by his standards. The treatment is topical, not chronological.

Binkley, Wilfred E. The Man in the White House: His Powers and Duties. Revised edition. New York, 1964). A handy treatment that should be used along with

Binkley, Wilfred E. President and Congress. 3rd revised edition. New York, 1967*.

Brown, Stuart Gerry. The American Presidency: Leadership, Partisanship, and Popularity. New York, 1966*. The subtitle reveals an apparent tendency to equate all three presidential qualities.

Corwin, Edward S. The President: Office and Powers. 4th edition. New York, 1957*. Still a classic that defines the constitutional role of Presidents.

Heller, Francis H. The Presidency: A Modern Perspective. New York, 1960*. In addition to five sprightly chapters dealing with "What We Expect," "What We Provide," "How and Whom We Select," "The Powers of the Office" and "The Measure of the Job," Professor Heller sets down a personal guide to reading on "The Presidency." This original study is a valuable contribution to the Random House Series in Political Science.

Hyman, Sidney. The American President. New York, 1954, is a valuable and authoritative study that explores the nature of the Presidency, the qualifications needed to fill it, and its growth into somewhat a unique institution in the free world. Particularly valuable is the author's examination of the man in the White House as Chief Executive, political leader, keeper of the national conscience, commander of a great coalition, master of ceremonials, patriotic symbol and national scapegoat.

Kane, Joseph Nathan. Facts About the Presidents. New York, 1960*. A handy, comprehensive record of each President. It gives comparative and biographical data.

Koenig, Louis W. The Chief Executive. New York 1964. This authoritative study of presidential power can be studied with the same author's paperback volume.

Koenig, Louis W. Official Makers of Public Policy: Congress and the President. Glenview, Ill., 1967*.

Laski, Harold J. The American Presidency. New York, 1940*. A classic now available in paperback as a title in the University Library books published by Grosset and Dunlap, Inc., N.Y.

Long, J.C. The Liberal Presidents: A Study of the Liberal Tradition in the American Presidency. New York, 1948. Presents the thesis that from its beginning the United States has been a liberal enterprise. The volume makes an attempt to describe to what extent the Presidency has expressed or promoted the evolving phases of liberalism. Although the author neglects McKinley, the student of the office of the Presidency can profit by analyzing the first chapter entitled "Preview of the Liberal Tradition."

Neustadt, Richard E. Presidential Power. New York, 1964). A provocative analysis of the function and authority of the Presidency by a professor of government who served on Truman's White House staff and acted as special consultant to John F. Kennedy during the transition of 1960-61. Although the author concentrates on the Presidency since F.D.R., he discusses "weak" and "strong" Presidents, by demonstrating the dynamic interrelation of power and politics.

Rossiter, Clinton. The American Presidency. 2nd edition. New York, 1960)*. A useful study by a Cornell professor whose companion volume in paperback, Parties and Politics in America enjoys popularity.

Schlesinger, Arthur Meier. "Historians Rate United States Presidents," Life, XXV (November 1, 1948), 65ff.

Schlesinger, Arthur Meier. "Our Presidents: A Rating by Seventy-five Historians," New York Times Magazine, June 29, 1962, 12ff.

NAME INDEX

TITLES IN THE OCEANA
PRESIDENTIAL CHRONOLOGY SERIES
Reference books containing
Chronology—Documents—Bibliographical Aids
for each President covered.
Series Editor: **Howard F. Bremer**

1 **GEORGE WASHINGTON***
   edited by Howard F. Bremer
2 **JOHN ADAMS***
   edited by Howard F. Bremer
3 **JAMES BUCHANAN***
   edited by Irving J. Sloan
4 **GROVER CLEVELAND****
   edited by Robert I. Vexler
5 **FRANKLIN PIERCE***
   edited by Irving J. Sloan
6 **ULYSSES S. GRANT****
   edited by Philip R. Moran
7 **MARTIN VAN BUREN****
   edited by Irving J. Sloan
8 **THEODORE ROOSEVELT****
   edited by Gilbert Black
9 **BENJAMIN HARRISON***
   edited by Harry J. Sievers
10 **JAMES MONROE***
   edited by Ian Elliot
11 **WOODROW WILSON****
   edited by Robert I. Vexler
12 **RUTHERFORD B. HAYES***
   edited by Arthur Bishop
13 **ANDREW JACKSON****
   edited by Ronald Shaw
14 **JAMES MADISON****
   edited by Ian Elliot
15 **HARRY S TRUMAN*****
   edited by Howard B. Furer
16 **WARREN HARDING****
   edited by Philip Moran
17 **DWIGHT D. EISENHOWER*****
   edited by Robert I. Vexler
18 **JAMES K. POLK***
   edited by John J. Farrell

19 **JOHN QUINCY ADAMS***
   edited by Kenneth Jones
20 **HARRISON/TYLER*****
   edited by David A. Durfee
21 **ABRAHAM LINCOLN*****
   edited by Ian Elliot
22 **GARFIELD/ARTHUR*****
   edited by Howard B. Furer
23 **WILLIAM McKINLEY**
   edited by Harry J. Sievers
24 **ANDREW JOHNSON**
   edited by John N. Dickinson
25 **WILLIAM HOWARD TAFT**
   edited by Gilbert Black
26 **CALVIN COOLIDGE**
   edited by Philip Moran

Available Soon

27 **JOHN F. KENNEDY**
   edited by Ralph A. Stone
28 **THOMAS JEFFERSON**
   edited by Arthur Bishop
29 **TAYLOR/FILLMORE**
   edited by John J. Farrell
30 **LYNDON B. JOHNSON**
   edited by Howard B. Furer
31 **FRANKLIN D. ROOSEVELT**
   edited by Howard F. Bremer
32 **HERBERT HOOVER**
   edited by Arnold Rice

* 96 pages, $3.00/B
** 128 pages, $4.00/B
*** 160 pages, $5.00/B